Alastair Sawday's

Special Places to Stay

Scotland

First edition

Published in October 2008

Alastair Sawday Publishing Co. Ltd,
The Old Farmyard, Yanley Lane,
Long Ashton, Bristol BS41 9LR, UK
Tel: +44 (0)1275 395430
Fax: +44 (0)1275 393388
Email: info@sawdays.co.uk
Web: www.sawdays.co.uk

The Globe Pequot Press,
P. O. Box 480, Guilford,
Connecticut 06437, USA
Tel: +1 203 458 4500
Fax: +1 203 458 4601
Email: info@globepequot.com
Web: www.globepequot.com

Design concept: Company X, Bristol
Maps: Maidenhead Cartographic Services
Printing: Scotprint, Haddington
UK distribution: Penguin UK, London

ISBN-13: 978-1-906136-14-7

A catalogue record for this book is available from the British Library.

Cover design: Company X, Bristol.
Cover photo credits. Thanks to:
1. britainonview/Steve Lewis 2. David George/Redcover.com 3. Jean Maurice/Redcover.com
Photo right: www.istockphoto.com

Contents

The buildings

Beautiful as they were, our old offices leaked heat, used electricity to heat water and rooms, flooded spaces with light to illuminate one person, and were not ours to alter. So in 2005 we created our own eco-offices by converting some old barns to create a low-emissions building. Heating and lighting the building, which houses over 30 employees, now produces only 0.28 tonnes of carbon dioxide per year. Not bad when you compare this with the 6 tonnes emitted by the average UK household. We achieved this through a variety of innovative and energy-saving building techniques, described below.

Insulation We went to great lengths to ensure that very little heat will escape, by:

• laying insulating board 90mm thick immediately under the roof tiles and on the floor

• lining the whole of the inside of the building with plastic sheeting to ensure air-tightness

• fixing further insulation underneath the roof and between the rafters

• fixing insulated plaster-board to add another layer of insulation.

All this means we are insulated for the Arctic, and almost totally air-tight.

Heating We installed a wood-pellet boiler from Austria, in order to be largely fossil-fuel free. The pellets are made from compressed sawdust, a waste product from timber mills that work only with sustainably managed forests. The heat is conveyed by water to all corners of the building via an under-floor system.

Water We installed a 6000-litre tank to collect rainwater from the roofs. This is pumped back, via an ultra-violet filter, to the lavatories, showers and basins. There are two solar thermal panels on the roof providing heat to the one (massively insulated) hot-water cylinder.

Lighting We have a carefully planned mix of low-energy lighting: task lighting and up-lighting. We also installed three sun-pipes – polished aluminium tubes that reflect the outside light down to chosen areas of the building.

Electricity All our electricity has long come from the Good Energy Company and is 100% renewable.

Photo: Tom Germain

Materials Virtually all materials are non-toxic or natural. Our carpets, for example, are made from (80%) Herdwick sheep-wool from National Trust farms in the Lake District.

Doors and windows The doors are wooden, double-glazed, beautifully constructed in Norway. Old windows have been double-glazed.

We have a building we are proud of, and architects are fascinated by. But best of all, we are now in a better position to encourage our owners and readers to take sustainability more seriously.

What we do

Besides moving the business to a low-carbon building, the company works in a number of ways to reduce its overall environmental footprint:

- all office travel is logged as part of a carbon sequestration programme, and money for compensatory tree-planting is dispatched to SCAD in India for a tree-planting and development project
- we take the train for business trips wherever possible; when we have to fly, we 'double offset'
- recycled cooking oil is used in one company car and LPG in the other
- organic and Fair Trade basic provisions are used in the staff kitchen and organic food is provided at all in-house events
- all kitchen waste is composted and used on the office organic allotment.

Our total 'operational' carbon footprint (including travel to and from work, plus our trips to visit our Special Places to Stay) is just over 17 tonnes per year. We have come a long way, but we would like to get this figure as close to zero as possible.

Alastair Sawday Publishing – a green company

For many years Alastair Sawday Publishing has been 'greening' the business in different ways. Our aim is to reduce our environmental footprint as far as possible – with almost everything we do we have the environmental implications in mind. (We once claimed to be the world's first carbon neutral publishing company, but are now wary of such claims). In recognition of our efforts we won a Business Commitment to the Environment Award in 2005, and in 2006 a Queen's Award for Enterprise in the Sustainable Development category. In that year Alastair was voted ITN's 'Eco Hero'.

We have created our own eco-offices by converting former barns to create a low-emissions building. Through a variety of innovative and energy-saving techniques this has reduced our carbon emissions by 35%. But becoming 'green' is a journey and, although we began long before most companies, we still have a long way to go.

In 2008 we won the Independent Publishers Guild Environmental Award. The judging panel were effusive in their praise, stating: "With green issues currently at the forefront of publishers' minds, Alastair Sawday Publishing was singled out in this category as a model for all independents to follow. Its efforts to reduce waste in its office and supply chain have reduced the company's environmental impact, and it works closely with staff to identify more areas of improvement. Here is a publisher who lives and breathes green. Alastair Sawday has all the right principles and is clearly committed to improving its practice further."

Our Fragile Earth series is a growing collection of campaigning books about the environment. Highlighting the perilous state of the world yet offering imaginative and radical solutions and some intriguing facts, these books will make you weep and smile. They will keep you up to date and well armed for the battle with apathy.

08 ipa Independent Publishing Awards

THE QUEEN'S AWARDS FOR ENTERPRISE: SUSTAINABLE DEVELOPMENT 2006

I proposed marriage on the top of a Scottish hill, in the Campsies. Those hills had always lingered in my memory, for my mother grew up at their feet and had spoken of them with a passion that Scots seem to draw on easily. You only have to mention Robert the Bruce, Robbie Burns or Loch Lomond and the eyes grow misty; dreaming begins. Don't even begin on Mary Queen of Scots. Perhaps the burghers of Basingstoke feel the same way about home, but the Scots have a rich store of nostalgia and it lies close to the surface.

(Those of you with a name-ist sense of humour will be glad to know that Scotland was first united under a king called Kenneth and grew to its present size under another called Malcolm. Neither name curdles the blood.)

Centuries of battling fiercely for their independence, and against each other, have kept the steel in the velvet Scots. They played a big role in the creation and running of the Empire. I remember reading of the relief of Lucknow by a Scottish regiment that had marched rapidly through the Indian heat for hundreds of miles – probably in their heavy kilts. I've learned to think tenderly and admiringly of Scotland.

Your very first contact will reveal the special qualities of the Scots, for in conversation, replying to a casual question about directions, a rare gentleness emerges. They wield a charm as penetrating as that of the Irish, using manners more elegant than is now common. This, and the astonishing loveliness of the countryside, are what will lure you back. You will be lured by other things too, such as the mighty

Photo: Tom Germain

Edinburgh Festival in August, one of the first great modern festivals and still the liveliest. There is also a lively art scene in Glasgow, and both cities have a cultural vigour that seems to grow by the year. You might go for the handsome castles, the ruined abbeys of the Borders, or the gardens that are nourished by so much helpful rain, the fishing, the walking – even the ski-ing. However, it will be the people that capture your affections. They will bring you back.

This book will create encounters with some fine people. It is not just their houses that we have selected, it is the owners themselves; for are they not the heart and soul of their houses? The same applies to the hotels within these pages. They are inspired by their hoteliers, all individuals with determination and character, not by hotel-and-catering-trained managers with no heart in it. We launched our books on a wave of disillusion with mass tourism; we offered something very different: character, authenticity, terrific value and a dash of panache. All those things are here in Scotland in rich abundance.

This is our first book on Scotland alone. It is a gem, as tightly packed with sheer pleasure as a bottle of Scotch. Mix the two and your view of the country and its people will change forever.

Alastair Sawday

You could explore Scotland for a lifetime and be constantly inspired. Stay in our carefully selected special places and you'll meet generous hosts eager to help you discover their fascinating regions and keen to have you taste their fine food; we hope you'll leave refreshed and determined to visit again.

Kate Ball, Editorial Co-ordinator

Photo right: Forter Castle, entry 121
Photo left: Chlenry Farmhouse, entry 34

It's simple. There are no rules, no boxes to tick. We choose places that we like. We also recognise that one person's idea of special is not necessarily someone else's so we try to give a variety of places, and prices. We take huge pleasure in finding people and places that do their own thing – brilliantly; places that are unusual and follow no trends; places of peace and beauty; people who are kind and interesting – and genuine.

Beautiful scenery, fabulous food, generous people and history in hatfuls

Inspections

We visit every place to get a feel for how it ticks. We don't take a clipboard and we don't have a list of what is acceptable and what is not. Instead, we chat for an hour or so with the owner or manager and look round. It's all very informal, but it gives us an excellent idea of who would enjoy staying there. If the visit happens to be the last of the day, we sometimes stay the night. Places are then revisited regularly so that we can keep things fresh and accurate.

Photo left: Ardanaiseig, entry 13
Photo right: Inwood, entry 63

Feedback

In between inspections we rely on feedback from our readers, as well as from staff members who are encouraged to visit places across the series. This feedback is invaluable to us and we always follow up on comments. We like your recommendations, too. So please stay in touch and tell us about your experiences and your discoveries. You can use the feedback form in this book (page 181) or on our website at www.sawdays.co.uk.

Occasionally misunderstandings occur, even with the best of intentions. So if your bedroom is cold or the bedside light is broken, please don't seethe silently and write to us a week later. Say something to the owners at the time. They will be keen to put things right if they can.

Subscriptions

Owners pay to appear in our guides. Their fees go towards the high costs of inspecting, of producing an all-colour book and of maintaining our website. We only include places and owners that we find positively special. It is not possible for anyone to buy their way into our guides.

Disclaimer

We make no claims to pure objectivity in choosing our Special Places. They are here because we like them. Our opinions and tastes are ours alone and this book is a statement of them; we hope that you will share them. We have done our utmost to get our facts right but apologise unreservedly for any mistakes that may have crept in.

You should know that we do not check such things as fire alarms, swimming pool security or any other regulation with which owners of properties receiving paying guests should comply. This is the responsibility of the owners.

Photo left: Monachyle Mhor, entry 125
Photo right: Skirling House, entry 130

Finding the right place for you

Our descriptions are carefully written to help you steer clear of places that will not suit you, but lead you instead to personal paradise. So read between the lines: what we don't say is sometimes as important as what we do.

Wherever you choose to stay, remember that the owners are experts at knowing their patch. They can often recommend secret beaches, excellent restaurants, super walks and gardens to visit – occasionally ones that aren't usually open to the public. Some places may provide maps and a bus timetable; some owners may be happy to pick you up at the end of a long walk. Do ask.

On the B&B pages you will find a huge variety of places, and also owners: some will be hovering with freshly baked cake when you arrive, others may be out shopping for your supper, having left a key under a stone. Mostly these are people's homes; you will encounter family life and its attendant chaos in some, and complete privacy in others, while a fair number of owners will be happy for you to stay all day.

For those who prefer more anonymity, there are many wonderful hotels, some child-friendly, others more suited to those who prefer peace and quiet. A sprinkling of deeply spoiling hotels will keep the fashionistas happy, while there are family-run and comfortingly old-fashioned places for traditionalists. There are also gorgeous self-catering places, some classically contemporary, a few crisply chic, many simple but cosy. Choose from dreamy wilderness boltholes for two, sweet cottages for families, or magnificent castles for larger gatherings.

Photo left: Broad Bay House, entry 149
Photo right: West Holmhead Cottage, Craig Farm, entry 39

Maps

Each property is flagged with its entry number on the maps at the front. These maps are the best start to planning your trip, but you'll need a proper road map for real navigation. Most places will send you detailed instructions once you have booked your stay.

It's simple. There are no rules, no boxes to tick. We choose places that we like.

Symbols

Below each entry you will see some symbols, which are explained at the very back of the book. They are based on information given to us by owners. However, things do change: bikes may be under repair or WiFi may have been added. Please use the symbols as a guide rather than an absolute statement of fact. Owners occasionally bend their own rules, so it is worth asking if you may take your child or dog, even if the entry doesn't have the symbol.

Photo: Beinn Bhracaigh, entry 117

Children – The symbol is given to owners who accept children of any age. It does not mean they will necessarily have cots, highchairs, safety equipment etc, so do check. If an owner welcomes children but only those above a certain age, this is stated at the end of the description. Even these folk may accept your younger child if you are the only guests. Many who say no to children do so not because they don't like them but because they may have a steep stair, an unfenced pond or they find balancing the needs of mixed age groups too challenging.

Pets – The symbol is given to places where your pet can sleep in your bedroom but not on the bed. Be realistic about your pet – if it is nervous or excitable or doesn't like the company of other dogs, people, chickens or children, then say so.

Quick reference indices

At the back of the book (page 182) we list those places:

- suitable for wheelchair users
- within 2 miles of a National Cycle Network route.

Rooms

We tell you if bedrooms are doubles, twin/double (ie. with zip and link beds), suite (with a sitting area), family or single. Most owners are flexible and can often juggle beds or bedrooms; talk to them about what you need before you book. Most bedrooms in our B&Bs and hotels have an en suite bath or shower room; we only mention bathroom details when they do not. Please check with owners for bathroom details for self-catering places.

Meals

In B&Bs and hotels a full cooked breakfast is included in the room price, unless we say otherwise. Obviously if you have chosen to self-cater, you must organise your own. Many of our hotels offer a half-board option, and some of our B&Bs will arrange an evening meal on request.

Bookings and cancellations

Requests for deposits vary; some are non-refundable, and some owners may charge you for the whole of the booked stay in advance.

Photo: Assynt House, entry 83

Some cancellation policies are also more stringent than others. Some will charge you the total cost if you cancel at short notice. If they hold your credit card details they may deduct a cancellation fee from it and not contact you to discuss this. So ask owners to explain their cancellation policy clearly before booking so you understand exactly where you stand; it may well help you avoid a nasty surprise.

Payment

All our owners take cash and UK cheques with a cheque card. Those who also take credit cards have the appropriate symbol.

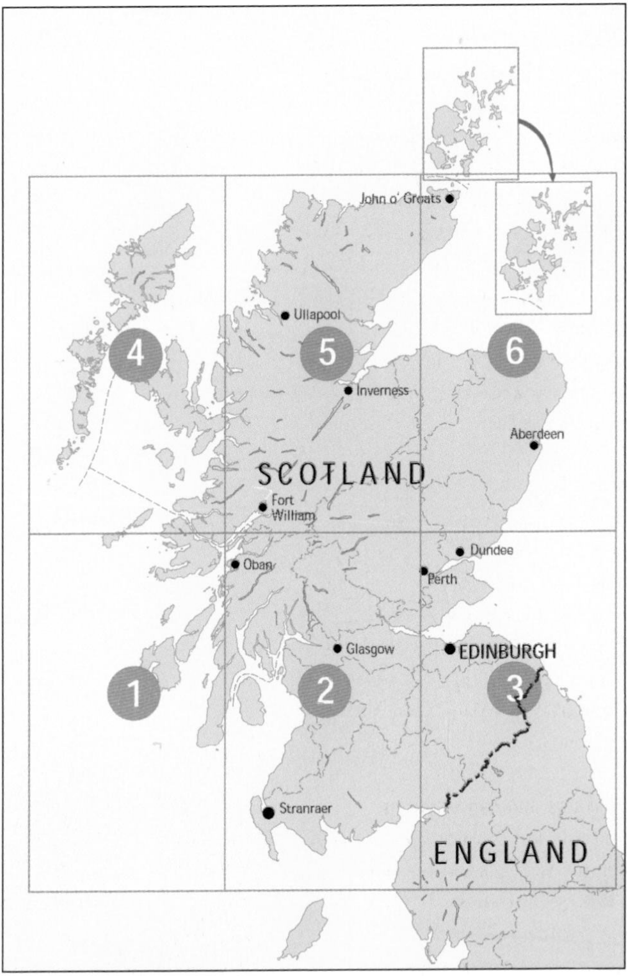

©Maidenhead Cartographic, 2008

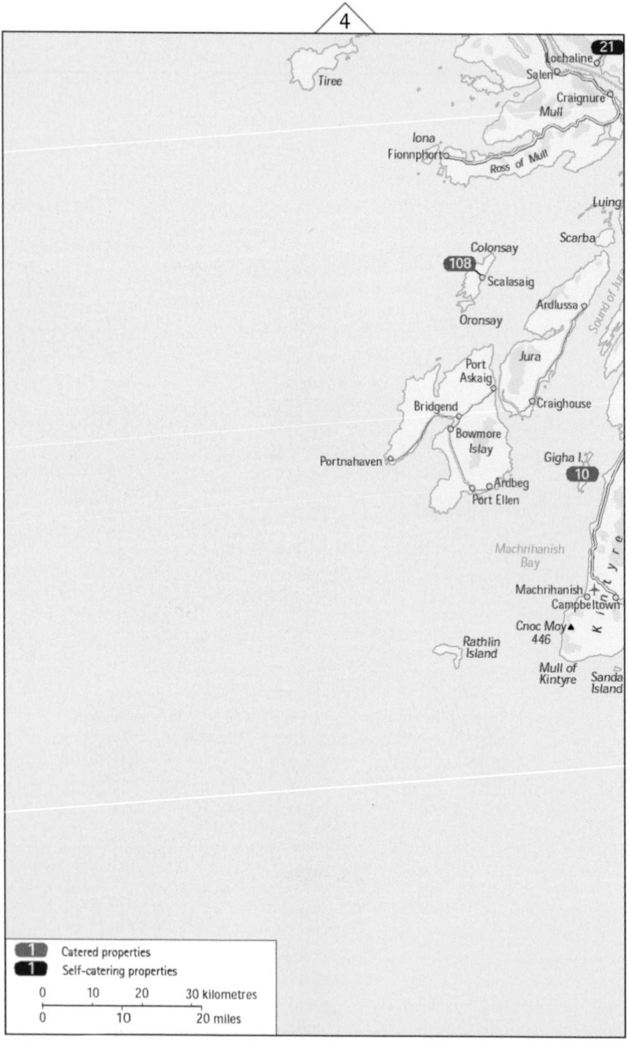
4
21
Lochaline
Salen
Tiree
Craignure
Mull
Iona
Fionnphort
Ross of Mull
Luing
Scarba
Colonsay
108
Scalasaig
Ardlussa
Sound of Jura
Oronsay
Jura
Port Askaig
Bridgend
Craighouse
Bowmore
Islay
Portnahaven
Gigha I.
10
Ardbeg
Port Ellen
Machrihanish Bay
Kintyre
Machrihanish
Campbeltown
Cnoc Moy
446
Rathlin Island
Mull of Kintyre
Sanda Island
1 Catered properties
1 Self-catering properties
0 10 20 30 kilometres
0 10 20 miles

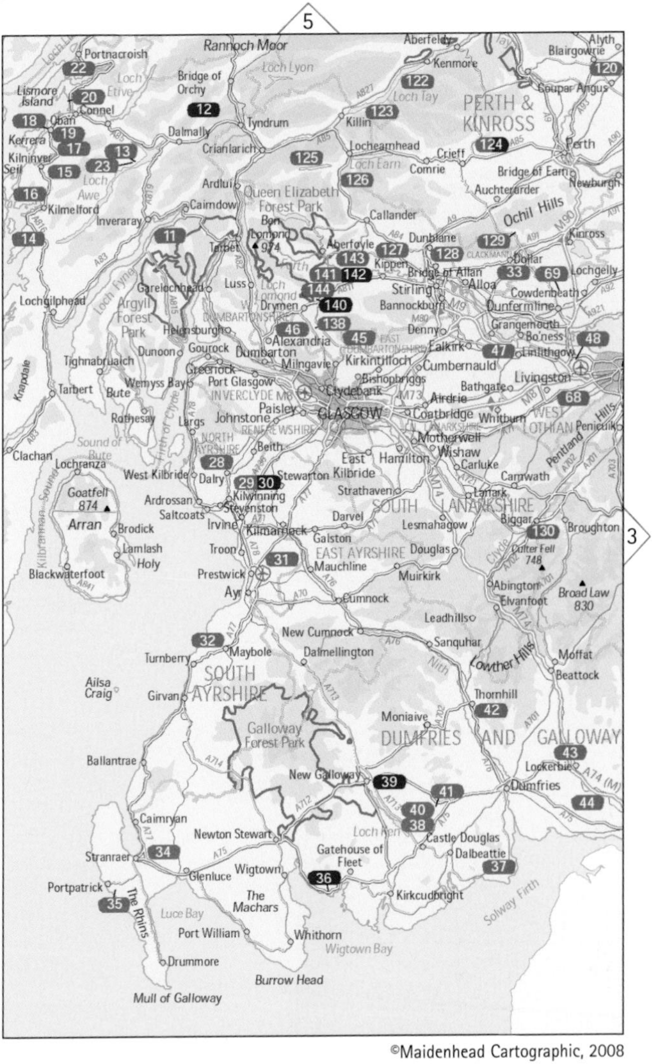

©Maidenhead Cartographic, 2008

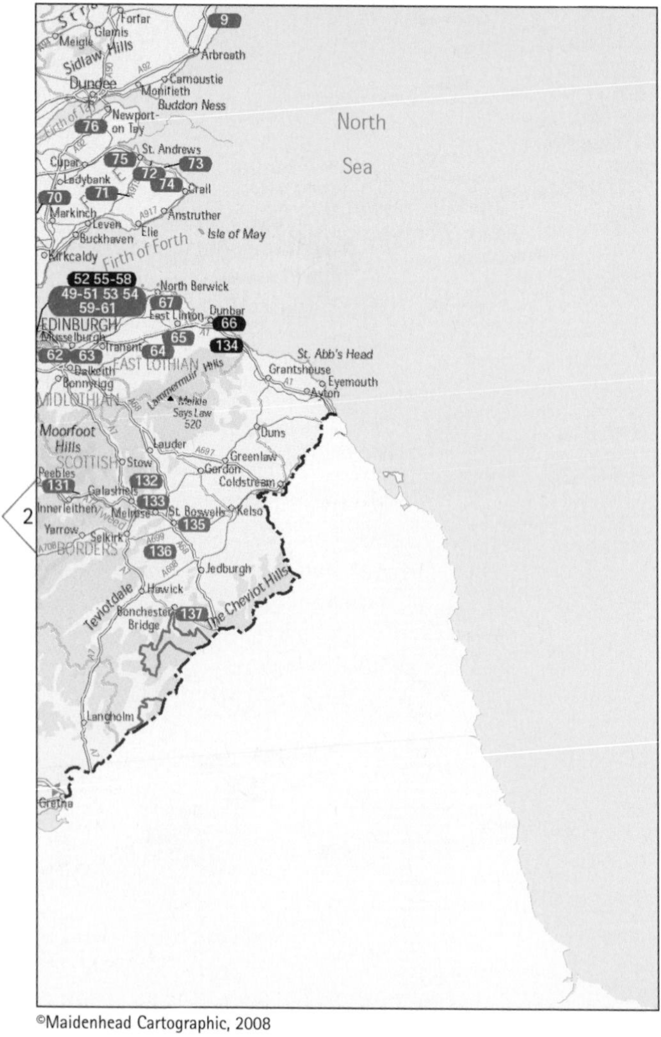

©Maidenhead Cartographic, 2008

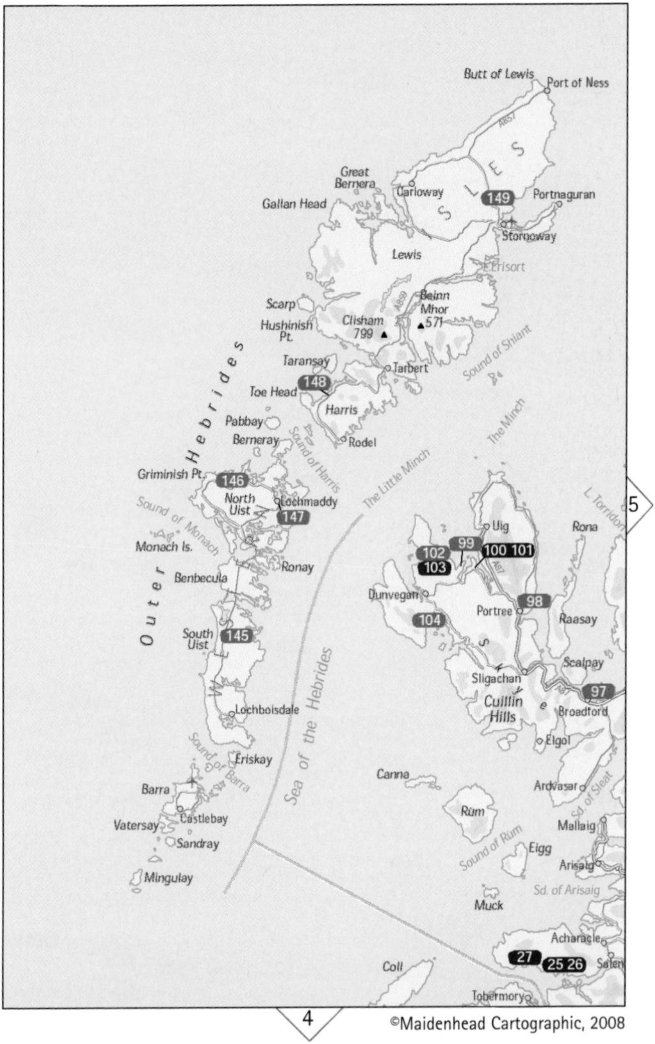

©Maidenhead Cartographic, 2008

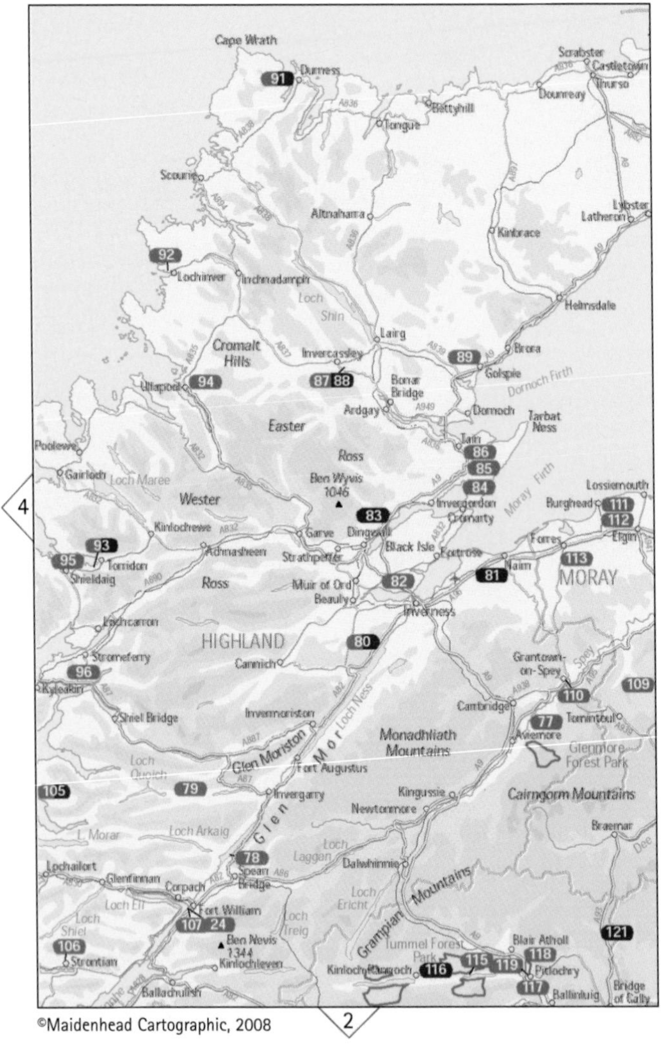
Cape Wrath
Durness
91
Scrabster
Castletown
Thurso
Dounreay
Bettyhill
Tongue
A836
A838
A9
A897
Scourie
A894
Altnaharra
Lybster
Latheron
Kinbrace
92
Lochinver
Inchnadamph
Loch Shin
Helmsdale
Lairg
Cromalt Hills
Invercassley
A839
89
Brora
Golspie
87
88
Ullapool
94
Bonar Bridge
Dornoch Firth
Ardgay
A949
Dornoch
Tarbat Ness
Easter Ross
A835
A832
Poolewe
Tain
86
85
Gairloch
Loch Maree
Ben Wyvis 1046
84
Moray Firth
Lossiemouth
Wester Ross
Invergordon
Burghead
111
112
83
Cromarty
Kinlochewe
Garve
Dingwall
Elgin
93
95
Achnasheen
Black Isle
Forres
Torridon
Strathpeffer
Fortrose
113
Shieldaig
Nairn
81
MORAY
Muir of Ord
82
Beauly
Inverness
Lochcarron
HIGHLAND
80
Stromeferry
Grantown-on-Spey
Cannich
96
Spey
Kyleakin
109
110
Loch Ness
Carrbridge
Shiel Bridge
Invermoriston
77
Tomintoul
Monadhliath Mountains
Aviemore
Glen Moriston
Glenmore Forest Park
Loch Quoich
Fort Augustus
105
79
Invergarry
Kingussie
Cairngorm Mountains
Newtonmore
Glen Mor
Braemar
L. Morar
Loch Arkaig
Dee
78
Loch Laggan
Lochailort
Spean Bridge
Dalwhinnie
Glenfinnan
Corpach
Loch Eil
Fort William
Loch Ericht
Grampian Mountains
Loch Shiel
107
24
Loch Treig
121
Ben Nevis 1344
Blair Atholl
106
Tummel Forest Park
115
118
Strontian
Kinlochleven
116
119
Kinloch Rannoch
Pitlochry
Ballachulish
117
Ballinluig
Bridge of Cally
4
2

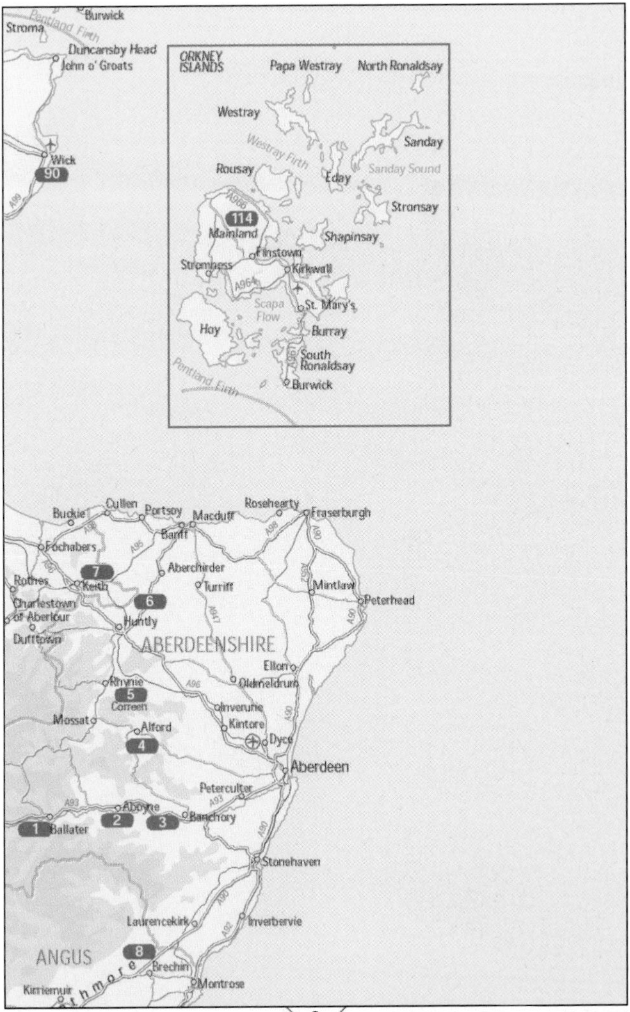
Stroma
Burwick
Pentland Firth
Duncansby Head
John o' Groats
Wick
90
A99
ORKNEY ISLANDS
Papa Westray
North Ronaldsay
Westray
Westray Firth
Sanday
Sanday Sound
Rousay
Eday
Stronsay
A966
114
Mainland
Shapinsay
Finstown
Stromness
Kirkwall
A964
Scapa Flow
St. Mary's
Hoy
Burray
A961
South Ronaldsay
Pentland Firth
Burwick
Cullen
Buckie
Portsoy
Macduff
Rosehearty
Fraserburgh
Banff
A98
A90
Fochabers
A95
Aberchirder
A952
7
Rothes
Keith
Turriff
Mintlaw
6
Peterhead
Charlestown of Aberlour
A947
Huntly
Dufftown
ABERDEENSHIRE
Ellon
Rhynie
A96
Oldmeldrum
5
Correen
Inverurie
Mossat
Kintore
Alford
4
Dyce
Aberdeen
Peterculter
A93
Aboyne
2
3
Banchory
1
Ballater
Stonehaven
Laurencekirk
Inverbervie
A92
ANGUS
8
Brechin
Kirriemuir
Strathmore
Montrose

3

Scotland

Photo: istockphoto

Darroch Learg

The country here is glorious – walk by Loch Muick, climb Lochnagar, fish the Dee or drop down to Braemar and the highland games. This is a smart family-run hotel firmly rooted in a graceful past, an old country house with tartan fabrics hung on walls, roaring fires, polished brass, Zoffany wallpaper and good food in an admired restaurant. Bedrooms come in different shapes and sizes; all have warmth and comfort in spades. Big grand rooms at the front thrill with window seats, wallpapered bathrooms, old oak furniture, perhaps a four-poster. Spotlessly cosy rooms in the eaves are equally lovely, just not quite as big. A perfect highland retreat.

Price	£140-£210. Half-board (obligatory May-Sept, & Saturdays all year) £110-£140 p.p.
Rooms	12: 10 twins/doubles, 2 four-posters.
Meals	Sunday lunch £24. Dinner, à la carte, about £45. 7-course tasting menu £55.
Closed	Christmas week & last 3 weeks in January.
Directions	From Perth, A93 north to Ballater. Entering village, hotel 1st building on left above road.

Nigel & Fiona Franks
Braemar Road, Ballater AB35 5UX
Tel 01339 755443
Web www.darrochlearg.co.uk

Lys-na-Greyne House

Peace, tranquillity and a natural welcome – one of the loveliest places. Expect a sweeping stair, sun-streamed rooms, log fires, a country-house feel and the most comfortable beds in Scotland. Your room may be huge – two are; one with a dressing room and a balcony, all with family antiques, bathrobes, fine linen, Spode china... and views of river, field, forest and hill where osprey and lapwing glide. Meg picks flowers and organic veg from the garden and her food is delicious; David is an enthusiastic naturalist and can advise on walking and wildlife. Nearby, golf, fishing and castles by the hatful.

Price	£90. Singles from £45.
Rooms	3: 1 twin/double; 2 twins/doubles with separate bath/shower. Extra shower available.
Meals	Supper £25. Pub/bistro 15-minute walk.
Closed	Rarely.
Directions	From Aboyne, A93 west for Braemar. Just before 30mph sign, left down Rhu-na-Haven Rd. House 400 yds on, 4th gateway on right.

David & Meg White
Rhu-na-Haven Road, Aboyne AB34 5JD
Tel 01339 887397
Email meg.white@virgin.net

Woodend House

Elegant riverside living at a fishing lodge by the river Dee – one of the most magnificent settings in Scotland. Outside, a wild, wonderful garden; inside, beautiful wallpapers, fabrics and rugs. The dining hall leads to the kitchen with an Aga, the drawing room has dreamy river views, the large bedrooms ooze comfort and more fabulous views, and the bathrooms have old cast-iron baths and fine toiletries. Breakfast and dinner are local, seasonal and first-class. All this, and a fishing hut and a secure rod room for salmon and sea trout fishing in season. *Minimum stay two nights.*

Price	£100. Singles £75.
Rooms	3: 1 double, 1 twin; 1 twin with separate bath.
Meals	Dinner, 4 courses, £30. Packed lunch £5-£10. Pub 2 miles.
Closed	Christmas, New Year & occasionally.
Directions	Directions on booking.

Miranda & Julian McHardy
Trustach, Banchory AB31 4AY

Tel 01330 822367
Web www.woodend.org

Lynturk Home Farm

The stunning drawing room, with pier-glass mirror, ancestral portraits and enveloping sofas, is reason enough to come, while the food, served in a candlelit, deep-sage dining room, is delicious, with produce from the farm. You're treated very much as friends here and your hosts are delightful. It's peaceful, too, on the Aberdeenshire Castle Trail. The handsome farmhouse has been in the family since 1762 and you can roam the surrounding 300 acres of rolling hills. Inside, good fabrics and paints, hunting prints and some lovely family pieces. "A blissful haven," says a reader. *Fishing, shooting & golf breaks.*

Price	From £80. Singles £50.
Rooms	3: 2 twins/doubles; 1 double with separate bath.
Meals	Dinner, 4 courses, £25. Pub 1 mile.
Closed	Rarely.
Directions	20 miles from Aberdeen on A944 (towards Alford); thro' Tillyfourie, then left for Muir of Fowlis & Tough; after Tough, 2nd farm drive on left, signed.

John & Veronica Evans-Freke
Alford AB33 8DU

Tel 01975 562504
Email lynturk@hotmail.com

Ford of Clatt

A perfect, and peaceful, retreat for writers, artists and anybody wishing to hide away. Lucy and her family have a lovely, 19th-century former drovers' inn with an atmosphere of quiet serenity, tucked in below the Correen hills. Your bedroom is a warm, comfortable sanctuary with family photos, a spotted teapot, books and fresh flowers on antique tables; chill out on a striped sofa stool, watch the view from the cane chairs by the window or loll in a roll top with L'Occitane soaps. Breakfast is hearty, perfect for walkers, and there are interesting megalithic standing stones; Lucy offers massage to yomp-weary limbs.

Price	£60. Singles £42.
Rooms	1 twin/double.
Meals	Packed lunch on request. Pub/restaurants within 2 miles.
Closed	Rarely.
Directions	From Aberdeen A96. 7 miles after Invervrie left at Oyne fork. After Oyne, left to Clatt. After Leslie T-junc, house on corner on right; turn into courtyard.

Lucy Aykroyd
Clatt, Huntly AB54 4PJ

Tel	01464 831115
Web	www.fordofclatt.co.uk

Old Mayen

Follow narrow lanes crowded by beech trees and hedges, through high rolling hills and fast flowing rivers to this beautiful house perched next to a farm and overlooking the unspoilt valley below. You get classic country-house style in elegant bedrooms, spoiling bathrooms, a book-filled sitting room, cut flowers and a delicious candlelit dinner by a roaring fire. Fran and Jim are infectiously enthusiastic and kind; breakfasts are a moveable feast (outside in good weather) and the garden hums with birds. A fine retreat for tired and jaded souls – and there are castles, distilleries and gardens to visit.

Price	£80. Singles £45.
Rooms	2: 1 double; 1 double with separate shower.
Meals	Dinner £25. Supper £18. Packed lunch £8.
Closed	Rarely.
Directions	From A96, A97 to Banff. After crossing river Deveron (9 miles), left onto B9117; 3 miles, on left behind thick beech hedge.

James & Fran Anderson
Rothiemay, Huntly AB54 7NL
Tel 01466 711276
Email oldmayen@tiscali.co.uk

Balwarren Croft

Thirty acres at the end of a farm track, a field of Highland cattle, mixed woodland, ancient dykes, a lochside full of birdlife, a herb garden with over 200 varieties and a burn you may follow down the hill. Hazel and James, warm, friendly, quietly passionate about green issues, came to croft 25 years ago. The whole place is a delight: cathedral roof, shiny wooden floors, cashmere blankets, sparkling bathrooms, log fires, delicious breakfasts (home eggs, jams and chutneys) and dinner is a treat. A beautiful, uplifting place in an area steeped in mystery – and peace. *Courses in dry stone walling & all things herbal.*

Price	£68-£74. Singles £40-£46.
Rooms	2: 1 twin; 1 double.
Meals	Dinner, 3 courses, £22. Pub/restaurant 10 miles.
Closed	Rarely.
Directions	North from Aberchirder on B9023. Right at Lootcherbrae (still B9023); 2nd left for Ordiquhill. After 1.7 miles, right at farm track opp. Aulton Farm; last croft up track.

Hazel & James Watt
Ordiquhill, Cornhill AB45 2HR
Tel 01466 751688
Web www.balwarren.com

Newtonmill House

The house and grounds are in apple-pie order; the owners are charming and unobtrusive. This is a little-known part of Scotland, so explore the glens, discover deserted beaches and traditional fishing villages, and play a round or two of golf on one of the many good courses nearby. Return to a cup of tea in an elegant sitting room, then a proper supper of seasonal, local and home-grown produce. Upstairs are crisp sheets, soft blankets, feather pillows, fresh flowers, homemade fruit cake and sparkling, warm bathrooms with thick towels; you are beautifully looked after here.

Price	£96-£110. Singles from £60.
Rooms	2: 1 twin; 1 double with separate bath.
Meals	Dinner, 4 courses, from £28. Supper, 2 courses, from £18. BYO. Packed lunch £10. Pub 3 miles.
Closed	Christmas.
Directions	Aberdeen-Dundee A90, turning marked Brechin/Edzell B966. Heading towards Edzell, Newtonmill House is 1 mile on left, drive marked by pillars and sign.

Rose & Stephen Rickman
Brechin DD9 7PZ
Tel 01356 622533
Web www.newtonmillhouse.co.uk

Ethie Castle

Amazing. A listed Pele tower that dates to 1300 and which once was home to the Abbot of Arbroath, murdered in St Andrews on Henry VIII's orders. His private chapel remains, as does his secret stair. As for the rest of the house: turret staircases, beautiful bedrooms, a 1500s ceiling in the Great Hall, a Tudor kitchen with a walk-in fireplace that burns night and day. Kirstin and Adrian are experts at breathing new life into old houses and have already started to reclaim the garden. Lunan Bay, one of Scotland's most glorious beaches, is at the end of the road. There's a loch too.

Price	From £95. Singles from £75.
Rooms	3: 1 four-poster; 1 twin/double, 1 double, each with separate bath/shower.
Meals	Dinner, 4 courses with wine, £30. Packed lunch up to £10. Pub/restaurant 3 miles.
Closed	Rarely.
Directions	From Arbroath N. on A92; right after Shell garage for Auchmithie; left at T-junc.; on for 2 miles; at phone box, private road to Ethie Barns in front.

Adrian & Kirstin de Morgan
Inverkeilor, Arbroath DD11 5SP

Tel	01241 830434
Web	www.ethiecastle.com

Achamore House

No traffic jams here, tucked between the mainland and Islay. Despite its grandeur – turrets, Arts & Crafts doors, plasterwork ceilings – Achamore is not stuffy and neither is Don, your American host. A coastal skipper, he can take you to sea, or over to other islands in his diesel catamaran. Find warm wood panelling and light-washed rooms, huge bedrooms with shuttered windows, oversize beds, heavy antiques; all have iPods and music. You get the run of the house – billiard room, library, large lounge, TV room (great for kids). With 50 acres of gardens and a quiet beach it's ideal for big parties or gatherings.

Price	£90-£130. Singles from £35.
Rooms	9: 2 doubles, 1 family room; 2 doubles sharing bath; 2 twins/doubles sharing bath; 2 singles sharing bath.
Meals	Pub/restaurant 1 mile.
Closed	Rarely.
Directions	Uphill from ferry landing, turn left at T-junc.; 1 mile, stone gates on right, signed; house at top of drive.

Don Dennis
Isle of Gigha PA41 7AD

Tel 01583 505400
Web www.achamorehouse.com

The Lodge

You are in Campbell country! Follow the rambling road around Loch Fyne to this elegant Victorian shooting lodge with an ancient oak woodland in its grounds. Enter a grand, enormously high ceilinged entrance hall, horned animals keeping watch from their lofty mantle. The house is a treasure trove... of mahogany bookcases and portraits in gold frames, candelabras, tapestries and open period fireplaces. Fall asleep over a copy of Dickens (no TV signal here!) beneath a coronet canopy, wake refreshed for a highland stroll with a hamper from Loch Fyne Oysters: pâté, smoked salmon, oatcakes, a bottle of wine.

Price	£80. Singles £60.
Rooms	1 double with separate bath.
Meals	Packed lunch or hamper £15-£20. Restaurants 5 miles. Oyster bar 7 miles.
Closed	Rarely.
Directions	From Glasgow on A83, left on A815 to St Catherine's. Train station: Arrochar, 11 miles.

Mr & Mrs Michael Thorndyke
St Catherine's, Loch Fyne PA25 8AZ

Tel 01499 302208
Email lauri.thorndyke@btinternet.com

The Old House

For six miles the leafy track hugs the rushing river. Salmon leap and pine tower above. (As the train from London chugs into Bridge of Orchy, why not leave the car behind and let your lovely hosts collect you?). The house, once the Earl of Breadalbane's sporting lodge, has been renovated with flair: the sitting room has a railway-sleeper mantelpiece, there's a four-poster on the ground floor (two twins are upstairs), and a 'wet room' with a vast shower. A pretty, secluded garden has decking for meals outside, and walkers are spoilt for choice: take a stroll, or climb 2,500 feet up Ben Udlaidh for views to the islands.

Price	£350-£1,000 per week.
Rooms	House for 6 (8 with sofabed): 1 four-poster; 2 twins.
Meals	Hotel 4 miles.
Closed	Never.
Directions	Directions given on booking.

John & Erica Kerr
Arichastlich, Glen Orchy PA33 1BD
Tel 01838 200399
Web www.glen-orchy.co.uk

Ardanaiseig

You're lost to the world, ten miles down a track that winds past giant rhododendrons before petering out at this baronial mansion. Beyond, Loch Awe rules supreme. In one of the loveliest hotel drawing rooms (gold leaf panelling, Doric columns rising gleefully) an enormous window frames the view. There are roaring fires wherever you go, eccentric art and a lawned terrace that runs down to the loch. Country-house bedrooms are the real thing (old armoires, feather boa lamp shades, the odd four-poster), and there's a funky suite with a glass wall opening out to a terrace. Dinner is a seven-course feast – as one might expect of this flamboyant hotel.

Price	£122-£404. Boathouse £252-£404. Singles from £91. Half-board £108-£233 p.p.
Rooms	18: 8 twins/doubles, 7 doubles, 2 four-posters, 1 boathouse suite.
Meals	Light lunch from £4. Afternoon tea £2-£10. Dinner, 7 courses, £45.
Closed	2 January-8 February.
Directions	A85 to Taynuilt. Left onto B845 for Kilchrenan. Left at Kilchrenan pub; down track for 4 miles.

Peter Webster
Kilchrenan, Taynuilt PA35 1HE
Tel 01866 833333
Web www.ardanaiseig.com

Corranmor House

A radiant setting on the Ardfern peninsula. Barbara and Hew are as generous and committed to their guests as they are to the 400-acre farm, where they rear sheep and geese. The drawing room started life as a 16th-century bothy (you'd never guess!), the red dining room sparkles with silver, they enjoy dining with guests and the food is delicious: goose, mutton, lamb, or fish from local landings. Bedrooms are exceptionally private – the double across the courtyard, the suite with the log-fired sitting room. Wander and admire; the eye always comes to rest on the water and boats of Loch Craignish and the Sound of Jura.

Price	£80. Suite £80-£135. Singles £45.
Rooms	2: 1 double & sitting room; 1 family suite & sitting room.
Meals	Lunch £15. Dinner, 3 courses and cheese, £30; with lobster £45. Pubs/restaurants 0.75 miles.
Closed	1 December-3 January; 4th week of August.
Directions	From A816, B8002 to Ardfern, & through village; 0.75 miles past church, long white house high on right. Right by Heron's Cottage, up drive.

Hew & Barbara Service
Ardfern, Lochgilphead PA31 8QN
Tel 01852 500609
Email corranmorhouse@aol.com

Melfort House

Enter a wild landscape of hidden glens, ancient oak woods and rivers that tumble to a blue sea. Find a Georgian-style, beautifully renovated house with views straight down the loch, exquisite furniture, designer fabrics, oak flooring and original paintings and prints. Bedrooms are sumptuous, with superb views (especially the Loch room with its Art Deco bathroom in viridian green), soft carpets, warmth and comfort. Yvonne and Matthew (who cooks) are brilliant at looking after you; breakfast on fresh fruit, Stornoway black pudding, tattie scones fresh from the Aga – even chilli omelettes! Argyll at its finest.

Price	£85-£115. Singles from £65. £15 for sofabed.
Rooms	3: 1 double, 2 twins/doubles.
Meals	Dinner, 3 courses, from £26. Packed lunch £7. Pub/restaurant 400 yds.
Closed	Rarely.
Directions	From Oban take A816 south, signed Campbeltown. After 14 miles, go thro' Kilmelford, then right to Melfort. Follow road & bear right after bridge.

Yvonne & Matthew Anderson
Kilmelford, Oban PA34 4XD

Tel 01852 200326
Web www.melforthouse.co.uk

Glenmore

A pleasing buzz of family life and no need to stand on ceremony. The house was built in 1854 but it's the later 30s additions that set the style: carved doorways, red-pine panelling, Art Deco pieces, oak floors, elaborate cornicing and a curvy stone fireplace. Alasdair's family has been here for 140 years and much family furniture remains. One of the huge doubles is arranged as a suite with a single room and a sofabed; bath and basins are chunky 30s style with chrome plumbing. From the organic garden and the house there are magnificent views of Loch Melfort with its bobbing boats; you're free to come and go as you please.

Price	£70-£90. Singles £40-£50.
Rooms	2: 1 family suite; 1 double with separate bath/shower.
Meals	Pub 0.5 miles, restaurant 1.5 miles.
Closed	December & January.
Directions	From A816 0.5 miles south of Kilmelford; a private tree lined avenue leads to Glenmore. House signed from both directions. Go past Lodge House at bottom of drive; follow drive for 0.25 miles.

Melissa & Alasdair Oatts
Kilmelford, Oban PA34 4XA
Tel 01852 200314
Web www.glenmorecountryhouse.co.uk

Barndromin Farm

Jamie and Morag run the farm – and three children, two collies, one kelpie, a clutch of hens and Frank the cat. It's a busy home, and a happy one, that opens its arms to guests. Bedrooms are carpeted and comfy, with flowery duvets and pretty family pieces, there's a big red sofa in the drawing room and a polished table for breakfast – tuck into croissants, bacon, sausages, black pudding, farm eggs. As for the views: the farmhouse, in the family for 100 years, is set on the hillside overlooking the glassy loch. Fish, walk, ride, spot grouse, sheep, cows, deer, red squirrels and rare butterflies. Gorgeous.

Price	From £70.
Rooms	3: 1 double, 1 twin, 1 double with private bath.
Meals	Pub/restaurant 4-6 miles.
Closed	Never.
Directions	6 miles south of Oban on A816 to Lochgilphead. 2nd entrance on left 200 yds after Knipoch Hotel.

Jamie & Morag Mellor
Knipoch, Oban PA34 4QS
Tel 01852 316297
Web www.knipochbedandbreakfast.com

The Manor House

A 1780 dower house for the Dukes of Argyll, high on the hill, with views over Oban harbour to the Isle of Mull. A smart and proper place, not one to bow to the fads of fashion: sea and harbour views from the lawn, a fire roaring in the drawing room, a beautiful tiled floor in the hall, an elegant bay window in the dining room. Bedrooms tend to be small but pretty and come in warm colours with fresh flowers, crisp linen, bowls of fruit and good bathrooms. Try Loch Fyne kippers for breakfast, salmon for lunch, rack of lamb for supper; there's excellent home baking, too. See the day's close from McCaig's Folly; sunsets here are special. *Children over 12 welcome.*

Price	£115-£185. Half-board £87.50-£122.50 p.p.
Rooms	11: 9 doubles, 2 twins.
Meals	Lunch from £8.50. Dinner, 5 courses, £36.
Closed	Christmas.
Directions	In Oban, follow signs to ferry. Hotel on right 0.5 miles after ferry turn-off, signed.

Ann MacEachen
Gallanach Road, Oban PA34 4LS
Tel 01631 562087
Web www.manorhouseoban.com

Lerags House

Drive down a single-track road through lochs and gentle mountains to this handsome late-Georgian house near the water. Bedrooms are light-filled and lovely – pale earthy colours, big beds with Italian linen, a suite with a view to the loch: Charlie and Bella bring style, friendliness, good prices, great service and Bella's exceptional food. The delightful garden runs down to tidal mud flats; watch the ebb and flow from the dining room while you breakfast on proper porridge. At the end of the road is a beach for walks or a constitutional dip. Day trips to Mull, Crinan and Glencoe are all easy, all wonderful. The Glasgow–Oban sea plane flies daily. *Arrival after 4pm.*

Price	Half-board £90-£100 p.p. Singles from £110.
Rooms	6: 4 doubles, 1 twin/double, 1 suite.
Meals	Half-board only. Packed lunch £8.
Closed	Christmas.
Directions	From Oban, south on A816 for 2 miles, then right, signed Lerags for 2.5 miles. House on left, signed.

Charlie & Bella Miller
Lerags, Oban PA34 4SE
Tel 01631 563381
Web www.leragshouse.com

Dun Na Mara

Twenty paces from the door, past the standing stone, a sweep of private beach and – on a clear day – dazzling views to Mull. The Arts & Crafts house has been given a minimalist makeover by Mark and Suzanne – ex-architects and friendly, caring, interesting hosts. The result is a luminous interior of low-slung beds, quilted throws, cream bucket chairs, sensual bathrooms, colourful cushions and sea views from three bedrooms. Breakfast on banana and walnut porridge, kedgeree, the full Scottish works; end the day with sherry in the sitting room, magazines, DVDs, beautiful art and books. *Children over 12 welcome.*

Price	£90-£105. Singles £50-£65.
Rooms	7: 5 doubles, 2 singles.
Meals	Pubs 3 miles.
Closed	December-January.
Directions	North from Oban on A828; over Connel Bridge; north for two miles; house signed left just after lay-by, before Benderloch village.

Mark McPhillips & Suzanne Pole
Benderloch, Oban PA37 1RT

Tel 01631 720233
Web www.dunnamara.com

Ardtornish

Golden eagles have been seen soaring, as have sea eagles; otter, pine martens and deer roam the estate. There's nothing out of place, no crime and no pollution – you'll feel not a twinge of stress. This is a heavenly spot, far from everything, yet the big house and its buildings are an isle of civilisation in 60 square miles of wilderness. Scattered among the main Victorian house and its estate houses and cottages are the 'special places' – some vast, almost baronial, others more cosy and separate; some are modernised, others not. At the end of the loch is the Sound of Mull – a vast playground for lovers of the outdoors. A delight.

Price	£345-£1,600 per week. Please call for details.
Rooms	Victorian mansion house, estate houses & cottages. 12 units in total.
Meals	Pub/restaurant 2 miles.
Closed	Never.
Directions	Directions given on booking.

John Montgomery
Morvern, Oban PA34 5UZ

Tel 01967 421288
Web www.ardtornish.co.uk

The Airds Hotel & Restaurant

Faultless service, ambrosial food and cosy interiors make this one of Scotland's most indulging country-house hotels. Views slide down to Loch Linnhe and cross to the towering mountains of Ardnamurchan. A small conservatory, candlelit at night, frames it perfectly, and in good weather you can skip over the lane to a pretty garden with tables and parasols. Pre-dinner drinks are in the sitting rooms – open fires, elegant sofas, fresh flowers, books; formal dinners are served on Limoges china. Retire to smart bedrooms (crisp florals, soft colours, Frette linen, Italian bathrobes) to find your bed turned down and the curtains drawn. Bliss.

Price	Half-board £245-£415 for two. Cottage £560-£1,600 per week inc. breakfast.
Rooms	11 + 1: 4 doubles, 4 twins, 3 suites. 1 cottage for 2-4.
Meals	Half-board only (except cottage). Lunch £5-£25. Dinner for non-residents, £49.50.
Closed	2 days a week, November-February.
Directions	A82 N. for Fort William; A828 S. for Oban. Right for Port Appin after 12 miles. On left after 2 miles.

Shaun & Jenny McKivragan
Port Appin, Appin PA38 4DF

Tel 01631 730236
Web www.airds-hotel.com

Sithe Mor House

Terrific views from this lovely house on the shores of Loch Awe; its own bay and jetty below, acres of sky above and a winning pair at the helm. Patsy ensures all runs smoothly and John, a former oarsman of repute and the first man to row each way across Scotland, sweeps you along with joie de vivre. With ornate plasterwork, antlers and oils, lofty domed ceilings in the bedrooms and loch views, this 1880s house combines a baronial feel with massive luxury in bathrooms, beds and fabrics. Stay for dinner, borrow a kilt, marvel at the Oxford and Cambridge boat race memorabilia. *Minimum stay two nights.*

Price	£100-£110. Singles £60-£75.
Rooms	2: 1 double, 1 twin/double.
Meals	Dinner, 4 courses, £35. Restaurants & pub 0.5-3 miles.
Closed	Rarely.
Directions	A82 from Glasgow; A85 from Tyndrum. At Taynuilt, left onto B845 to Kilchrenan village. After 1 mile, single track 'No Through Road' to Taychreggan. House is last on left.

Patsy & John Cugley
Kilchrenan, Loch Awe PA35 1HF

Tel	01866 833234
Web	www.sithemor.com

The Lime Tree

The Lime Tree is unique – an art gallery with rooms. The house, a Mackintosh manse, dates back to 1850, while the tree itself was planted in 1700. Inside is a small, stylish world – of stripped floors, bold colours, open fires, beautiful windows for views of Loch Linnhe. Airy bedrooms are delightful – oatmeal carpets, crisp white linen, good art, flat-screen TVs – and there's a rustic bistro for homemade soups, slow-cooked lamb, chocolate pudding. David – a mountain guide/stuntman who also paints – has a fabulous map room. If you want to do more than walk, climbing, cragging, mountain biking, kayaking and diving can all be arranged.

Price	£80-£110. Singles from £60.
Rooms	9: 4 doubles, 5 family.
Meals	Lunch, 3 courses, £10. Dinner, 3 courses, £25.
Closed	November.
Directions	North to Fort William on A82. Hotel on right at 1st roundabout in town.

David Wilson
Achintore Road, Fort William PH33 6RQ
Tel 01397 701806
Web www.limetreefortwilliam.co.uk

The Tower

Superb in any season: dreamy and remote. The tower is unusual, built by Richard on the corner of their house – beautifully done. From their woods have come ash for the little dining table, pine for the winding stair, oak for beams, logs for the wood-burner. There are simple chintz curtains, a deep tub in the bathroom, a fine circular room for the bed, a curved glass door to a small terrace and glorious views of Loch Sunart. Walk straight into the woods, onto the hillsides, into the waters of the loch. Borrow bikes for a day, pay for rucksack lunches, then come back to snooker, table tennis, a mini gym. Rugged and unspoiled.

Price	£380 per week.
Rooms	Tower for 2 (1 double).
Meals	Simple supper on arrival £5 per person.
Closed	Rarely.
Directions	Directions given on booking.

Lois & Richard Livett
Ardslignish, Acharacle PH36 4JG
Tel 01972 500201
Web www.selfcateringardnamurchan.co.uk

The Ruin

Over the lip of Loch Sunart, tucked into a land of old oak, asphodel and heather, crouches a place for two to roost. All is open plan: pad across heated tiles, bake bread in the kitchen, doze on the plump bed as the stillness of 80 acres descends. Logs, linen, games, an old film – all are yours – so settle by the wood-burner or on the terrace. And there's snooker, table tennis and a mini gym at the owners' house, a three-minute walk. Grab binoculars for guillemots, stride off for the mountains or shore, return to grill supper on the barbecue. Soothingly wild. *The Byre (sleeps two youngsters) can be let with The Ruin.*

Price	Ruin £410 per week. Byre £90 per week.
Rooms	Ruin for 2 (1 double). Byre for 2 youngsters (let to same party only).
Meals	Simple supper on arrival £5 per person.
Closed	Rarely.
Directions	Directions given on booking.

Lois & Richard Livett
Ardslignish, Acharacle PH36 4JG
Tel 01972 500201
Web www.selfcateringardnamurchan.co.uk

Taigh Na Cille

Be greeted by swirling skylarks, bobbing wagtails, sheep grazing on rough pastures that rise up from the Hebrides Sea. Your stone retreat is old Kilmory church, simply but cosily renovated. Oodles of mountain cabin charm comes from wooden floors, half wood-panelled walls, a log-burner and a cosy corner for eating (no TV: you're too remote). There are bunks on the ground floor and, on an open gallery above, slanting ceilings, skylights and a wood-framed king-size bed. Miles of coastal walks and sandy beaches surround you, sea and sky meet uninterrupted at the horizon, and views stretch out to the Isles of Eigg, Rhum, Muck and Skye.

Price	£250-£550 per week.
Rooms	Cottage for 4 (1 double; 1 room with bunkbeds).
Meals	Pub 5 miles.
Closed	Rarely.
Directions	Directions given on booking.

Jacqui Chapple
Kilmory PH36 4LH

Tel 01972 510262
Web www.steading.co.uk

Langside Farm

Your hosts' gentle intelligence and humour is reflected in their home – the main part dates back to 1745 – with long views to the east. Inside, a well-proportioned Georgian elegance, fresh contemporary artwork (some Elise's) and a snug Aga kitchen. Deep red sofas, pale striped walls, books and lamps draw you in; pretty bedrooms have a period feel and vary in style. Local (much organic) produce promises fine breakfasts and suppers; water comes from a private spring. There's good walking and golf nearby. Chat in the kitchen, sit by the fire, make yourselves truly at home.

Price	£59-£79. Singles from £36.50.
Rooms	3: 1 twin/double, 1 twin, 1 four-poster.
Meals	Packed lunch £5.50. Supper £15. Dinner £24.50. Pubs/restaurants 5-10 minute drive.
Closed	November, January & February.
Directions	Langside Farm is 0.7 miles from Dalry end of B784. B784 links B780 Dalry to Kilbirnie road to A760 Kilbirnie to Largs road.

Nick & Elise Quick
Dalry KA24 5JZ

Tel 01294 834402
Web www.langsidefarm.co.uk

The Carriage House

An avenue of limes, 250 acres of parkland, rhododendrons, wellingtonia – what a view to wake to! Luke's family have owned the estate and castle for 900 years. Their stylishly converted Carriage House, with its ochre walls, cobbled courtyard and drawing room, is full of light and comfortable good taste; polished floors, handsome antiques, family photographs, contemporary fabrics. Aga-cooked breakfasts are taken in a huge kitchen with hand-crafted fittings. Tennis court, swimming pool, country walks: this is an elegant place to unwind. The Borwicks are confident and keen hosts.

Price	£90. Singles £55.
Rooms	3: 1 double, 1 twin/double, 1 single/twin.
Meals	Pubs/restaurants 3-7 miles.
Closed	Rarely.
Directions	From Beith enter Dalry on A737. First left (signed Bridgend Industrial Estate); uphill through houses, past farm on right at top of hill. First right into Blair Estate.

Luke & Caroline Borwick
Blair, Dalry KA24 4ER

Tel 01294 833100
Web www.blairestate.com

The Stables Cottage

Sweep up an avenue of limes to the Blair Estate until the romantic Scottish castle comes into view. In its converted stables, in the east wing of the Carriage House, everything is set up for the great outdoors; leave sailing gear, walking boots and golf clubs downstairs, and plunge into a hot shower. Have a lazy family meal in the big kitchen, bag a spot by the fire in the lounge, or sneak off for a snooze – in straightforward bedrooms with floral curtains and carpeted floors. The Borwicks run one of the largest Rural Stewardship schemes in Ayrshire, protecting community woodlands, wetlands and hedges: all yours to explore.

Price	£450-£650 per week.
Rooms	Cottage for 5 (7 with sofabed): 1 double; 1 family room.
Meals	Pubs/restaurants 3-7 miles.
Closed	Never.
Directions	From Beith enter Dalry on A737. First left (signed Bridgend Industrial Estate); uphill through houses, past farm on right at top of hill. First right into Blair Estate.

Luke & Caroline Borwick
The Carriage House, Blair, Dalry KA24 4ER
Tel 01294 833100
Web www.blairestate.com

Heughmill

Five acres of fields and lawn with free-range hens that kindly donate for breakfast and huge views to the sea. The house is just as good, surrounded by old stone farm buildings, with climbing roses and a small burn tumbling through. Inside, a lovely country home with tapestries in an airy hall, an open fire in the sitting room and a terrace that sits under a vast sky. Country-house bedrooms are stylishly homely. Two have the view, one has an old armoire, another comes with a claw-foot bath; all have delightful art. Julia sculpts, Mungo cooks breakfast on the Aga. Rural Ayrshire waits, yet you are close to the airport.

Price	£65-£80.
Rooms	3: 2 twins/doubles, 1 twin.
Meals	Pubs within 2 miles.
Closed	Christmas & New Year.
Directions	3 miles south of Kilmarnock, turn east down B730 for Tarbolton. After 0.75 miles, right onto narrow road signed Ladykirk. House is 250 yds on right.

Mungo & Julia Tulloch
Craigie, Kilmarnock KA1 5NQ

Tel 01563 860389
Web www.stayprestwick.com

Culzean Castle

Culzean (pronounced 'Cullane') is one of Scotland's grandest buildings, a Robert Adam castle built into solid rock 200 feet above crashing waves. Country-house style rooms are either big or huge, with glowing fires, cashmere throws, twinkling chandeliers, thrilling sea views. Bathrooms are grandly traditional, service is thoughtful, the rest is awe-inspiring: portraits crammed on the walls, a sublime drawing room that juts out over the sea, an oval staircase with 12 Corinthian columns, an armoury of 716 pistols and 400 swords. Americans in search of ancestors will love it. Tour the castle before the tourists invade. Brilliant.

Price	£225-£375. Singles from £140. Whole floor £1,700 per night. Afternoon tea included.
Rooms	6: 1 double, 3 twins/doubles, 1 four-poster, all en suite; 1 twin/double with separate bath.
Meals	Dinner, 3 courses, £35. By arrangement.
Closed	Rarely.
Directions	From A77 in Maybole, A719 for 4 miles, signed.

Fi McClelland
The National Trust for Scotland,
Maybole KA19 8LE

Tel 01655 884455
Web www.culzeanexperience.org

Kennels Cottage

Live the dream: tour Scotland by classic car. Sandy does Triumphs, Austin Healeys, convertible Beetles. Tanya spoils you, with big crisp beds, huge white towels, elegant blinds, orchids and oriental touches. The old gamekeeper's cottage is a stunningly fresh, stylish and immaculate place, all white walls, white sofas, books, paintings and the odd flash of gold. In the morning, feast on local bacon, Fair Trade coffees and eggs from their hens served at one convivial table. Take a picnic to the garden, wander through what was the Dollarbeg estate, replete with pheasant and deer... totally unwind.

Price	£70-£80. Singles £50.
Rooms	3 doubles.
Meals	Packed lunch £10. Pub 2 miles.
Closed	January & February.
Directions	From Dollar take B913 towards Blairingone. House 2 miles from Dollar just before Blairingone.

Tanya Worsfold & Sandy Stewart
Dollarbeg, Dollar FK14 7PA
Tel 01259 742186/742476
Web www.guesthousescotland.co.uk

Chlenry Farmhouse

A wonderful approach, private and peaceful. Beyond the romantic old buildings in the glen and the rushing burn, the handsome house comes into view. It is a big traditional farmhouse full of old-fashioned comfort and fresh flowers, with charming owners and friendly dogs. In peaceful bedrooms, solid antiques jostle with tasselled lampshades, silk flowers and magazines on country matters; there are proper big bath tubs and suppers for walkers. Meals can be simple or elaborate, often with game or fresh salmon; gardens and golf courses wait to be discovered.

Price	£70. Singles from £45.
Rooms	3: 1 twin with separate bath; 1 double, 1 twin sharing bath.
Meals	Supper, £17.50. Dinner, 4 courses, £30. Packed lunch £6. Pub 1.5 miles.
Closed	Christmas, New Year & occasionally.
Directions	A75 for Stranraer. In Castle K., right opp. Esso station. Approx. 1.25 miles on, after right bend, right signed Chlenry. Down hill, 300 yds on left.

David & Ginny Wolseley Brinton
Castle Kennedy, Stranraer DG9 8SL

Tel 01776 705316
Web www.chlenryfarmhouse.com

Knockinaam Lodge

Lawns run down to the sea, sunsets streak the sky. This is an exceptional 1869 shooting lodge with unremitting luxuries: a Michelin star in the dining room, 150 malts in the bar and a level of service you might not expect in such far-flung corners. And history – Churchill once stayed and you can sleep in his room. This is very much a country house: expect plump cushions on a Queen Anne sofa in a morning room where the scent of flowers mixes with the smell of burnt wood... and invigorating cliff walks, curlews to lull you to sleep, nesting peregrine falcons and a rock pool where David keeps lobsters for the pot. Remote, beguiling, very spoiling.

Price	Half-board £95-£200 p.p. Singles from £165.
Rooms	10: 3 doubles, 6 twins/doubles, 1 suite.
Meals	Half-board only. Lunch, by arrangement, £25-£37.50. Dinner, 5 courses, included; non-residents £50.
Closed	Never.
Directions	From A77 or A75, signs for Portpatrick. 2 miles west of Lochans, left at smokehouse. Signed for 3 miles.

David & Sian Ibbotson
Portpatrick DG9 9AD
Tel 01776 810471
Web www.knockinaamlodge.com

Barholm Castle

Your chance to live in a castle: wind up a rough track to a creamy white building standing tall. The impressive Great Hall (your sitting room) has a huge fireplace and hand-painted ceiling, window seats for the views and underfoot heating to keep things cosy. Then it's down to the well-lit, vaulted kitchen – a fun place to gather and eat – and up a spiral stone stair to bed. The master room wows with a beamed ceiling and huge four-poster; its huge bathroom has a roll-top bath and a chaise longue. Climb on up to find more rooms and, at the very top, the Caphouse and the windswept parapet. Survey the land, all yours – at least for a week.

Price	£825-£1,150 per week.
Rooms	Castle for 7 + cot (2 four-posters; 1 twin; 1 single).
Meals	Pubs/restaurants 7 miles.
Closed	Rarely.
Directions	Directions given on booking.

Janet Inglis
Gatehouse of Fleet DG7 2EZ
Tel +31 70 5110775
Web www.barholm.net

Cavens

A welcoming country house that stands in six acres of native wood and sweeping lawns with views that stretch across a quilt of fields to the imperious Solway Firth. Inside, quietly elegant interiors flood with light; you get busts and oils, seagrass matting, golden sofas and smouldering fires. Angus whisks up delights single-handedly (perhaps scallops with lime and vermouth, bass with fennel, raspberry tartlets). Country-house bedrooms – some snug, others palatial – all have garden views. Lose yourself in beautiful country, play golf at spectacular Southerness. Afternoon tea can be eaten in the garden. A treat.

Price	£100-£160. Singles from £80.
Rooms	6: 5 doubles, 1 twin.
Meals	Dinner, 3 courses, £30. Packed lunch available.
Closed	House parties only December-February.
Directions	From Dumfries, A710 to Kirkbean (12 miles). Hotel signed in village, on left.

Jane & Angus Fordyce
Kirkbean DG2 8AA

Tel 01387 880234
Web www.cavens.com

Chipperkyle

Sink into the sofas without worrying about creasing them; this beautiful Scottish-Georgian family home has not a hint of formality, and the sociable Dicksons put you at your ease. Sitting and dining rooms connect through a large arch; there are family pictures, rugs on wooden floors and a log fire. Upstairs: a cast-iron bed dressed in good linen, striped walls, flowered curtains, lots of books and windows with views – this wonderful house just gets better and better. There are 200 acres, dogs, cats, donkeys and hens, and you can walk, play golf, visit gardens, sail or cycle – in magnificent countryside.

Price	£92.
Rooms	2: 1 double; 1 twin with separate bath/shower. Cot available.
Meals	Dinner available for groups. Pub 3 miles.
Closed	Christmas.
Directions	A75 Dumfries ring road for Stranraer. Approx. 12 miles to Springholm & right to Kirkpatrick Durham. Left at x-roads, after 0.8 miles, up drive on right by white lodge.

Willie & Catriona Dickson
Kirkpatrick Durham, Castle Douglas DG7 3EY
Tel 01556 650223
Web www.chipperkyle.co.uk

West Holmhead Cottage, Craig Farm

This forgotten corner of Scotland is blissfully empty – red squirrels, kites and otters are its reclusive residents. Among hills and forests is a bio-dynamic farm run by Richard and Mas; 450 acres flourish naturally, orchids, mushrooms, ancient woodland are pasture for cattle and sheep. Your spotless white-painted stone cottage (one of two on a quiet lane) has a down-to-earth feel that echoes the owners' values – furniture is simple but not cheap, beds are pine, walls creamy white. Books and fresh flowers welcome, local walks are described in detail on handwritten cards. To be surrounded by such raw beauty is a balm to every soul.

Price	£300-£500 per week.
Rooms	Cottage for 5 (1 double; 1 twin; 1 single).
Meals	Pub 4 miles.
Closed	Rarely.
Directions	Directions given on booking.

Mas Smyth & Richard Cunningham
Balmaclellan, Castle Douglas DG7 3QR
Tel 01644 420636
Web www.craigfarm.co.uk

Croys House

A wonderful old house in acres of parkland – grand but not forbidding. Inside, architectural styles slip effortlessly from Georgian to Victorian and your hosts have abounding energy; food is delicious, mostly home-reared, and served at an elegant polished table. Bedrooms are large and light with lovely views and good mattresses, bathrooms warm and generous – one has a rich maroon roll top. You are surrounded by a stunning garden with rolling lawns, impressive topiary, walled garden, sombre pond and dear little summer houses. Red squirrels quiver in the branches above you, kites soar and there is good fishing to be had. Lovely.

Price	£70. Singles £40.
Rooms	3: 1 double; 1 four-poster, 1 twin sharing bathroom (let to same party only).
Meals	Dinner £17.50.
Closed	Christmas & New Year.
Directions	3.5 miles from Castle Douglas. From town centre, A75 towards Dumfries. Left at Corsock sign. 2.5 miles from town centre, 1 mile along this road.

Alan & Patricia Withall
Bridge of Urr, Castle Douglas DG7 3EX
Tel 01556 650237
Web www.croys-house.co.uk

Craigadam

A 1703 house set in 700 acres, where pheasants strut proudly up the drive. The farmhouse becomes a 'country house' inside: a sitting room with three vast sofas and numerous chairs, a dining table that seats 26, seven rooms in the stables, three more in the house, a billiard room and an honesty bar. Delightful, energetic Celia pulls it all together and creates a house-party feel. The food and wines are fabulous and the lamb, venison, partridge and duck come from the family's organic farm. Retire to a themed bedroom (Scottish, African, Chinese), a deep soak and a comfortable bed.

Price	From £88. Singles on request.
Rooms	10 suites.
Meals	Dinner £25. Pub 2 miles.
Closed	Christmas & New Year.
Directions	A75, then north on A712 towards Corsock. After 2 miles, Craigadam signed on right.

Mrs Celia Pickup
Castle Douglas DG7 3HU

Tel	01556 650100
Web	www.craigadam.com

Trigony House Hotel

A super little hotel – warm, stylish and welcoming. Adam and Jan are doing their own thing wonderfully: delicious food, pretty rooms, a lovely garden. Inside: Japanese oak panelling in the hall, leather sofas in the sitting room and a fire in the dining room, where doors open onto the terrace for dinners in summer. Adam cooks delicious rustic fare; there's a vegetable garden that provides much in summer. Bedrooms are excellent value for money (some are dog-friendly) and come with summery florals, padded bedheads, golden throws. Falconry, riding and fishing can be arranged, even vintage car hire. Drumlanrig Castle is close and worth a peek.

Price	£90-£120. Suite £140. Single from £45. Half-board from £70 p.p.
Rooms	10: 8 twins/doubles, 1 single, 1 suite.
Meals	Lunch from £5. Dinner, 3 courses, £25.
Closed	24-26 & 31 December.
Directions	North from Dumfries on A76 through Closeburn. Signed left after 1 mile.

Adam & Jan Moore
Closeburn, Thornhill DG3 5EZ
Tel 01848 331211
Web www.countryhousehotelscotland.com

Applegarth House

Here is an old peaceful manse at the top of the hill, right next door to the church, with a 12th-century motte; the views from the pretty garden stretch for miles around. The house is a good size, with original pine floors and sweeping stairs. Off the large and light landing are three bedrooms with warm carpets, shuttered windows and glorious garden and country views. Let the tawny owls lull you to sleep then wake to freshly stewed fruits and excellent porridge. There are paths to wander through the flower beds, statues to admire and endless wildlife; a perfect stop off point for a trip north or south.

Price	£80-£84. Singles from £54.
Rooms	3: 2 twins; 1 double with separate bath.
Meals	Dinner £26. BYO. Hotel restaurant 1.5 miles.
Closed	Rarely.
Directions	M74 junc. 17 to Lockerbie, B7076 for Johnstonebridge. 1st right after 1.5 miles; after 100 yds left over m'way bridge. After 1 mile, right at T-junc., then 2nd left to church. Next to church.

Frank & Jane Pearson
Lockerbie DG11 1SX

Tel 01387 810270
Email jane@applegarthtown.demon.co.uk

Knockhill

Fabulous Knockhill: stunning place, stunning position, a country house full of busts and screens, oils and mirrors, chests and clocks, rugs and fires. In the intimate drawing room stuffed with treasures, floor-to-ceiling windows look down the wooded hill. Fine stone stairs lead to country-house bedrooms that are smart yet homely: headboards of carved oak or padded chintz, books and views. Come for a grand farming feel and delicious Scottish meals; the Morgans are the most unpretentious and charming of hosts. Mellow, authentic, welcoming – an enduring favourite.

Price	£80-£84. Singles £54.
Rooms	2: 1 twin; 1 twin with separate bath.
Meals	Dinner £26. Pub 5 miles.
Closed	Rarely.
Directions	From M74 junc. 19, B725 for Dalton. Right by church in Ecclefechan, signed Hoddam Castle. After 1.2 miles right at x-roads towards Lockerbie. 1 mile on, right at stone (not whitewashed) lodge cottage. At top of long drive.

Yda & Rupert Morgan
Lockerbie DG11 1AW

Tel 01576 300232
Email morganbellows@yahoo.co.uk

Finglen House

The Campsie Hills rise behind (climb them and you can see Loch Lomond), the Fin Burn takes a two-mile tumble down the hill into the garden, and herons and wagtails can be spotted from the breakfast table. All this 40 minutes from Glasgow. Sabrina's designer flair gives an easy, graceful comfort to the whole house: good beds in stylish rooms, proper linen, French touches, eclectic art, cast-iron baths and cream-painted wooden floors. A fresh, elegant drawing room with log fire is yours to share. Douglas, a documentary film maker, knows the Highlands and Islands well; he and Sabrina are fun and good company.

Price	£80. Singles £50.
Rooms	2: 1 double; 1 double with separate bath.
Meals	Pub 5-minute drive.
Closed	Christmas & New Year.
Directions	A81 from Glasgow right on A891 at Strathblane. 3 miles on, in Haughhead, look for a wall & trees on left, & turn in entrance signed Schoenstatt. Immed. left to house.

Sabrina & Douglas Campbell
Campsie Glen G66 7AZ

Tel 01360 310279
Web www.finglenhouse.com

Blairbeich Plantation

Past swaying birches to a Swedish wonderland in the woods. It is a beautiful fusion of antique and modern and a mini-loch laps three feet from its walls. There are light stone floors and cathedral ceilings and delightful ground-floor bedrooms that look onto the loch – an enclave of wilderness that universities come to study. Despite all this it is the interior that knocks you flat: Malla – relaxed, friendly, a fine cook – has covered every inch with something spectacular and the sitting room is a private art gallery. Mosaic showers, orchids, woodpeckers... and curling on the loch in winter. Fabulous.

Price	£70-£100. Singles from £60.
Rooms	2 doubles.
Meals	Dinner, 4 courses, £35. Pub/restaurant 1.5 miles.
Closed	Rarely.
Directions	From west, A811 into Gartocharn; 1st right (School Road); 1 mile up to T-junction, then left; house on right, signed.

Malla Macdonald
Gartocharn, Loch Lomond G83 8RR

Tel 01389 830257
Web www.blairbeich.com

Lochmill House

Susan is delightful and kind and spoils you rotten. Her home-baking is wicked (expect a feast for breakfast), her green fingers produce fresh flowers from a pretty, peaceful garden all year round, and she's hot on Scottish history so can help you make the best of your stay. The house is modern and on the edge of town, a mile or so from the M9 and very easy for Edinburgh and Glasgow. Big lovely rooms swim with light, there's a smart multi-windowed sitting room to relax in and a spotless country-cosy bedroom with wicker chairs and crisp linen. *Children over 12 welcome.*

Price	£75. Singles £40.
Rooms	1 twin.
Meals	Occasional supper/dinner. Packed lunch £6. Pub & restaurants 0.5 miles.
Closed	Christmas & occasionally.
Directions	From west M9, junc 4. From east M9 junc. 3, then A803 into Linlithgow. There, north onto A706 for Bo'ness & 0.2 miles on left. Follow to end of road.

Mr & Mrs W Denholm
3 Lade Court, Linlithgow EH49 7QF

Tel 01506 846682
Email susanedenholm@hotmail.com

Craigbrae

Half a mile down a narrow winding lane and you wash up at the old stone farmhouse, with huge windows overlooking fields and a cooperage across the yard. The house has been recently renovated so there's a lovely new bathroom in New England style and bedrooms that ooze tranquillity and thoughtful touches. Your hosts are hospitable and great fun; the drawing room is warm, cosy and homely; there are books, china, family pieces and good oils. Edinburgh is 15 minutes by train from the village, the airport 12 minutes by taxi or car. And there's a pretty garden that catches the sun.

Price	£70-£90. Singles from £35.
Rooms	3: 1 double; 2 twins/doubles sharing 2 bath/shower rooms.
Meals	Pubs/restaurants 2 miles.
Closed	Christmas.
Directions	Please ask for directions when booking.

Louise & Michael Westmacott
Kirkliston, Edinburgh EH29 9EL
Tel 0131 331 1205
Web www.craigbrae.com

11 Belford Place

Guests love Susan's modern townhouse above the Water of Leith. A golden retriever wags his welcome in the wooden-floored entrance, a picture-lined staircase winds upward. Outside, New Zealand flax bursts into flower while herons and foxes share an exquisite sloping garden. Handsome rooms offer china cups and floral spreads; dazzling bathrooms have Molton Brown goodies. Taste Stornoway black pudding at the gleaming breakfast table – there are simple suppers and box lunches if you're on the trot. You hear owls at night yet you're a hop from the city, with free parking and a bus stop nearby. *Minimum stay two nights in August.*

Price	£70-£120.
Rooms	3: 1 double, 2 twins/doubles.
Meals	Supper £10. Packed lunch £10. Pub 200 yds, restaurants 10-minute walk.
Closed	Christmas.
Directions	From city centre go to Belford Road; Belford Place is 1st left after Travelodge Hotel. House is down hill opposite Edinburgh Sports Club. Free parking. No 13 bus goes past top of lane.

Lady Susan Kinross
Edinburgh EH4 3DH

Tel 0131 332 9704
Web www.edinburghcitybandb.com

12 Belford Terrace

Leafy trees, a secluded garden, a stone wall and, beyond, a quiet riverside stroll. Hard to believe that Edinburgh's galleries, theatres and restaurants are a few minutes' walk. This Victorian end terrace, beside Leith Water, oozes an easy-going elegance, helped by Carolyn's laid-back but competent manner. Ground-floor bedrooms – she lives at 'garden level' – are big and creamy with stripy fabrics, antiques, sofas and huge windows. (The single has a *Boys Own* charm.) Carolyn spoils with crisp linen, books and biscuits and a delicious, full-works breakfast. After a day in town, relax in the garden.

Price	£60-£100. Singles from £40.
Rooms	3: 1 double, 1 twin/double; 1 single with separate shower.
Meals	Pub/restaurants within 10-minute walk.
Closed	Christmas.
Directions	From Palmerston Place through 2 sets of lights, downhill on Belford Rd past Menzies Belford Hotel. Immediately left is Belford Terrace.

Carolyn Crabbie
Edinburgh EH4 3DQ

Tel 0131 332 2413
Email carolyncrabbie@blueyonder.co.uk

21 India Street

Portraits of the Macpherson clan beam down upon you at delicious breakfast served in a sunny and elegant dining room. In this house of great character you are cared for by Zandra, who offers guests the Laird's Room with its half-tester and the (smaller) Patio Room with its own front entrance. And it's just a hop and a skip up the majestic cobbled streets of New Town to Princes Street and the centre. Zandra plays the Scottish harp, loves to cook, has two beautiful black labs and has written about her life as wife of a clan chieftain – read up about it all in the spacious drawing room.

Price	£95-£127.50. Singles £60-£85.
Rooms	2: 1 double, 1 twin.
Meals	Restaurants close by.
Closed	Rarely.
Directions	Down South Queensferry Rd; left at Y-junc; at 2nd Y-junc. left into Craig Leith Rd. Thro' Stockbridge, over lights at bridge; 3rd right into Royal Circus; sharp right thro' Circus Gdns; left into India St.

Mrs Zandra Macpherson of Glentruim
Edinburgh EH3 6HE
Tel 0131 225 4353
Web www.twenty-one.co.uk

The City Bothy

Here is a cool, contemporary studio flat. Unpromising, perhaps, at first glance, inside is another story. Brilliant use of space creates what feels like two rooms (bedroom and living room) out of one, while the design combines the most charming of old and new: a flat-screen TV, a 1940s kitchen larder, a wall-mounted head from some highland beast. Fair Trade teas and coffee, whisky and homemade biscuits greet you. Fifty yards off is Iglu, a lively organic restaurant; opposite is Kay's Bar, a deliciously small New Town pub. It's a five-minute walk to George Street, ten to Waverley Station – you couldn't be better placed for all that Edinburgh has to offer.

Price	£340-£600 per week (min. 3 nights).
Rooms	Studio for 2 (1 double).
Meals	Pubs/restaurants walking distance.
Closed	Rarely.
Directions	Directions given on booking.

Rhiannon Batten
Jamaica Mews, Edinburgh EH3 6HN
Tel 07976 729113
Web www.citybothy.com

7 Gloucester Place

A cantilevered staircase in walnut and mahogany, a soaring hand-painted cupola: the classic Georgian townhouse is five minutes from Princes Street. Rooms are cosy yet immaculate, sprinkled with paintings and decorative things from travels to far-flung places. Bedrooms are comfy, traditional and well-stocked with books and radio (and there are Z-beds for children). Bag the south-facing double with its stunning Art Deco bathroom and garden views. Naomi is pretty relaxed and happy to chat to you about the local music and art scene, or to leave you in peace. An interesting and hospitable place to unwind.

Price	£90-£110. Singles from £50.
Rooms	3: 1 double; 1 double with separate bath; 1 double with separate shower. Extra child beds.
Meals	Pubs/restaurants 300 yds.
Closed	Christmas & rarely.
Directions	From George St (city centre), down Hanover St, across Queen St at lights. Left into Heriot Row, right onto India St, then left.

Naomi Jennings
Edinburgh EH3 6EE
Tel 0131 225 2974
Web www.stayinginscotland.com

24 Saxe Coburg Place

A ten-minute walk – or an even quicker bus ride – from the centre of Edinburgh, this 1827 house stands in a quiet, no-through road with a communal garden in the centre. There's a garden level entrance to three simple and luxurious bedrooms with extra long beds, good lighting, handsome antiques and spotless bathrooms – one with Paris metro tiling in white and green. Most excitingly you can nip over the street in your bathrobe to the Victorian Baths for a swim, sauna or workout in the gym; all before a delicious, generous continental breakfast in the hall, or on the pretty terrace in summer. Marvellous.

Price	£75-£120. Singles £40-£55.
Rooms	3: 1 double, 1 twin/double, 1 single.
Meals	Continental breakfast. Restaurants/pubs 5-minute walk.
Closed	Rarely.
Directions	From George St, down Frederick St. Over 3 sets of lights, left at bottom of hill. Right up Clarence St; at junction, over to Saxe Coburg St. Saxe Coburg Place is at end. Ask about parking.

Diana McMicking
Edinburgh EH3 5BP

Tel 0131 315 3263
Web www.saxecoburgplace.co.uk

25 Saxe Coburg Place

You're in one of the city's classic New Town squares, all handsome terraces, private communal gardens and peace (no through road). Ignore the plain entrance hall and sweep through the inner door to your apartment on the ground floor – this is special! All the Georgian hallmarks are here: classic proportions, elegant shutters, deep window seats, gentle colours. Bathrooms are small but smart, bedrooms soft and comfortable, and the kitchen is a miracle of space-saving. Wake to morning views of the Botanic Gardens, then decide: galleries, museums, castle – or the shops and cafés of trendy Stockbridge? Live the dream. *Free parking at weekends.*

Price	£350-£1,190 per week (please call for nightly rates).
Rooms	Flat for 4 (6 with sofabed): 1 double; 1 twin/double.
Meals	Pubs/restaurants walking distance.
Closed	Rarely.
Directions	Directions given on booking.

Jane Slater
Edinburgh EH3 5BP
Tel 07711 826540
Web www.25saxecoburgplace.co.uk

London Street

This is classic New Town: wide cobbled streets, manicured communal gardens, houses one dreams of; now you can experience a slice of it. This lower ground-floor flat is elegantly sophisticated: fresh flowers, pale wood floors, an original fireplace, bright kilims, a well-crafted mix of old and new. There's a small kitchen decked out with every modern thing and a bathroom with floor-to-ceiling marble and mirrored alcoves softly lit. In the bedroom, one of Pippa's vintage travel cases folds out to reveal a set of drawers and hanging rail, and a generous window onto the garden creates a light, easy feel. Princes Street is a sprint away.

Price	£420-£650 per week.
Rooms	Flat for 2 (4 with sofabed): 1 double.
Meals	Pubs/restaurants walking distance.
Closed	Never.
Directions	Directions given on booking.

Pippa Lockhart
10 London Street, Edinburgh EH3 6NA
Tel 0131 556 0737
Web www.acklandedinburgh.co.uk

Pilrig House Apartments

Turn a corner to find a craggily handsome house overlooking parkland – Robert Louis Stevenson's family used to live here. The owners have created four delightful apartments (one theirs), with 18th-century proportions and a modern cottagey décor. In the Garden Apartment, the sunny living room and pretty, low-ceilinged kitchen sparkle with views of the garden or parkland; a cosy bedroom and pin-neat bathroom cosset with patchwork quilt, bathrobes, Scottish soaps. You'll want for nothing – binoculars, books, maps, welcoming whisky, fruit, chocolates. It's 15 minutes to Princes Street but the peace is supreme. *Reductions for weekly stays, please call for details.*

Price	Garden Apt £80-£150. Park & Balfour Apts £100-£170. (Prices are per night, min. 3 nights; highest rates are for Festival only).
Rooms	Garden Apt for 3. Park Apt for 4. Balfour Apt for 4.
Meals	Pubs/restaurants walking distance.
Closed	Never.
Directions	Directions given on booking.

Philip & Debbie Martin
30 Pilrig House Close, Edinburgh EH6 5RF

Tel 0131 554 4794
Web www.pilrighouse.com

Claremont Cottage Stables

Behind a huge wall is a charming, Georgian, ship's captain's house – and the Stables, your stylish, single-storey retreat. Step into the open-plan living room: fresh flowers, a sleek beige sofabed, a beautifully equipped kitchen in the corner. Delightful Sarah, the owner, is a professional chef and will stock your fridge if you ask. The light, airy bedroom has a comfy bed, white shelves for books, a super little shower – you'll sleep deeply for it's as quiet as can be. You may be a ten-minute walk from Leith and a short bus ride from Princes Street, but this feels like the country. *Secure parking available inside locked gates.*

Price	From £55 per night (min. 3 nights). £385-£600 per week.
Rooms	Cottage for 2 (4 with sofabed): 1 double.
Meals	Pubs/restaurants walking distance.
Closed	Never.
Directions	Directions given on booking.

Tom & Sarah Burnet
45 Claremont Road, Edinburgh EH6 7NN
Tel 0131 555 5585
Web www.claremontcottage.com

2 Fingal Place

An elegant house on a Georgian terrace. The leafy park lies opposite (look upwards to Arthur's Seat). Bustling theatres, shops and the university are a stroll away, yet this is a very quiet house. Your hostess is a Blue Badge Guide and will help plan your trips – or cater for celebrations and graduations with lunch and dinner; it's entirely flexible. Bedrooms are downstairs at garden level and have antique beds, spotless bathrooms and seductive linen; one looks onto a lovely patio garden. Noodle the Llasa Apso and Gillian's cat are equally welcoming. *Parking metered until 5.30pm weekdays, free at weekends.*

Price	£80-£115 (£90-£130 during Festival). Singles from £55 (from £65 during Festival).
Rooms	2: 1 twin (with single room attached), 1 twin.
Meals	Pubs/restaurants 100 yds.
Closed	22-27 December.
Directions	From centre of Edinburgh (West End), Lothian Rd to Tollcross (clock) & Melville Drive. At 2nd major lights, right into Argyle Place; immed. left into Fingal Place.

Gillian Charlton-Meyrick
The Meadows, Edinburgh EH9 1JX

Tel 0131 667 4436
Email gcmeyrick@fireflyuk.net

20 Blackford Road

A 20-minute stroll from the Royal Mile is a substantial Victorian house with relaxed hosts and a touch of old-world luxury. From a cushioned window seat you gaze onto a lovely wildlife-filled walled garden where you can eat out on a warm day; breakfasts, though not the full Monty, are superb. Bedrooms, one up, one down, are tranquil and serene, with delicately papered walls and lush toile de Jouy; the drawing room, with cream sofas, soft lights, drinks tray and beautiful books, is elegant yet cosy. Lucas the rescue greyhound completes the picture – of a happy, charming place to stay. *Minimum stay two nights in August.*

Price	£70-£90. Singles £60.
Rooms	2: 1 double/twin, 1 twin, each with separate bath.
Meals	Restaurants 500 yds.
Closed	Christmas & New Year.
Directions	A720 city bypass, take Lothianburn exit to city centre. Continue for 2.5 miles on Morningside Rd; right into Newbattle Terrace; 2nd left into Whitehouse Loan. Immed. right into Blackford Road. House at end on left.

John & Tricia Wood
Edinburgh EH9 2DS

Tel 0131 447 4233
Email jwood@dsl.pipex.com

1 Albert Terrace

A warm-hearted home with a lovely garden, an American hostess and two gorgeous Siamese cats. You are 20 minutes by bus from Princes Street yet the guests' sitting room overlooks pear trees and clematis and the rolling Pentland Hills. Cosy up in the winter next to a log fire; in summer, take your morning paper onto the terrace above the sunny garden. Books, fresh flowers, interesting art and ceramics and – you are on an old, quiet street – utter, surprising peace. Bedrooms are colourful, spacious and bright, one with an Art Deco bathroom and views over the garden. Clarissa is arty, easy, generous and loves having guests.

Price	£75-£85. Singles £35-£45.
Rooms	3: 1 double; 1 double, 1 single sharing bath.
Meals	Pubs/restaurants nearby.
Closed	Rarely.
Directions	From centre of Edinburgh, A702 south, for Peebles. Pass Churchill Theatre (on left), to lights. Albert Terrace 1st right after theatre.

Clarissa Notley
Edinburgh EH10 5EA

Tel	0131 447 4491
Email	canotley@aol.com

Inveresk House

Cromwell stayed here, and plotted his siege of Edinburgh Castle; the house oozes history. The magnificent main rooms are furnished with ornate antiques, squashy sofas in chintzes, flowers, gilt, mirrors, seriously gorgeous rugs and Alice's own vibrant art. Bedrooms and bathrooms, on the expected scale, come with vintage radiators, huge beds, good old-fashioned comfort. Musicians will be happy – there are two baby grands. Come for Inveresk (a conservation village), golf (the course at Musselburgh is the oldest in the world), interesting conversation and history by the hatful. Edinburgh is a bus hop away.

Price	£100-£140. Singles £65.
Rooms	3: 1 double, 1 twin, 1 family room.
Meals	Pubs/restaurants in Musselburgh.
Closed	Rarely.
Directions	From Edinburgh, A199 (A1) to Musselburgh. There, signs to Inveresk. At top of Inveresk Brae, sharp right into cul-de-sac. 2nd opening on right, opp. gates with GM on them, bear right past cottages to house.

Alice & John Chute
3 Inveresk Village, Musselburgh EH21 7UA
Tel 0131 665 5855
Web www.invereskhouse.com

Inwood

Lindsay and Irvine built this bungalow in 1983, minutes from the city centre yet surrounded by deep countryside within the Carberry Tower estate. Bedrooms have a light modern feel, comfortable chairs and garden views, laminated wood flooring in the bathrooms, cream and white linen and towels. A pretty conservatory opens to the garden, Lindsay's delight. She hands out leaflets about what is in flower to visitors, and you can buy plants too. Expect rambling roses in June and July, hydrangeas and rare exotics later on. In autumn, colchicums and tricyrtis; in spring, a woodland bursting with snowdrops, wood anemones, trilliums and 2,000 tulips.

Price	From £80. Singles from £50.
Rooms	2: 1 double, 1 twin.
Meals	Pub 1 mile.
Closed	Mid-January–mid-March.
Directions	From A1 Edinburgh to Berwick, off at 3rd exit. At traffic lights turn right on A6124 to Dalkeith. Follow signs to Carberry, left at A M Morrison sign; left at Inwood Garden sign.

Lindsay Morrison
Carberry, Musselburgh EH21 8PZ

Tel 0131 665 4550
Web www.inwoodgarden.com

Letham House

Sweep down the rhododendron-lined drive to enter a magical, secret world. This fine, early 17th-century mansion has elegant staircases, resplendent fabrics, gleaming antiques and roaring fires; generous, people-loving Barbara and Chris just want you to enjoy it all. They give you complete privacy and tranquillity in stunning south-facing bedrooms; the views over mature trees and impeccable parkland are the stuff of dreams. Eat robustly, sleep peacefully, indulge yourself in gorgeous bathrooms; this is a nurturing retreat. You won't want to leave, but there are beaches and golf nearby; Edinburgh is beyond.

Price	£90-£150. Singles £55-£75.
Rooms	5: 2 doubles, 2 twins/doubles; 1 suite with separate bath.
Meals	Dinner, 3 courses, £30. Packed lunch £10. Guest kitchen. Pubs/restaurants 1 mile.
Closed	Rarely.
Directions	From A1 south, exit at Oak Tree junction. Follow signs for Haddington (B6471). Immediately right after 40mph signs, through large stone pillars.

Barbara Sharman
Haddington EH41 3SS
Tel 01620 820055
Web www.lethamhouse.com

Eaglescairnie Mains

Wildlife thrives: eight acres of conservation headland have been created and wildflower meadows planted on this 350-acre working farm... you'd never guess Edinburgh is so close. The Georgian farmhouse sits in lovely gardens, its peace interrupted by the odd strutting pheasant. There's a traditional conservatory for summery breakfasts, a perfectly proportioned drawing room (coral walls, rich fabrics, log fire) for wintery nights, and beautiful big bedrooms full of books. Barbara is warm and charming, Michael's commitment to the countryside is wide-ranging, and the atmosphere is gracious and unhurried.

Price	£55-£75. Singles from £35.
Rooms	3: 2 doubles, 1 twin.
Meals	Pub 1 mile.
Closed	Christmas.
Directions	From A1 at Haddington B6368 south for Bolton & Humbie. Right immed. after traffic lights on bridge. 2.5 miles on through Bolton, at top of hill, fork left for Eaglescairnie. Entrance 0.5 miles on left.

Barbara & Michael Williams
Gifford, Haddington EH41 4HN
Tel 01620 810491
Web www.eaglescairnie.com

Hope Cottage

The little 1750 cottage was built of rich red sandstone to house local weavers – the old 'tron' for weighing fleeces still stands on the village green. All on one storey, rooms are not palatial but are stylish with a delightful feel – and children and dogs can frolic in a little patch of secluded garden. Heather, ever thoughtful, lives next door, and has maps and guides for jaunts. You can pluck herbs for your own cooking from her magical garden, which is open once a year as part of the Scottish Garden Scheme. There are golf courses in abundance, sandy beaches, glorious walks, and Edinburgh a half hour away.

Price	£400-£450 per week (please call for nightly rates).
Rooms	Cottage for 4 (1 double; 1 twin).
Meals	Pub 3 miles.
Closed	Never.
Directions	Directions given on booking.

Heather Allen
Stenton, Dunbar EH42 1TE
Tel 01368 850293

Glebe House

Gwen has lavished a huge amount of time and love on her 1780s manse. The perfect Georgian family house with all the well-proportioned elegance you'd expect, it is resplendent with original features – fireplaces, arched glass, long windows – that have appeared more than once in interiors magazines. Bedrooms are light, airy and hung with generous swathes of fabric. The sea is a stone's throw away and golfers have 21 courses to choose from. There's also a fascinating sea bird centre close by – yet you are 30 minutes from Edinburgh! Regular trains take you to the foot of the castle.

Price	£100. Singles by arrangement.
Rooms	3: 1 double, 1 twin, 1 four-poster.
Meals	Restaurants 2-minute walk.
Closed	Christmas.
Directions	From Edinburgh, A1 for Berwick. Left onto A198, follow signs into North Berwick. Right into Station Rd signed 'The Law', to 1st x-roads; left into town centre; house on left behind wall.

Gwen & Jake Scott
Law Road, North Berwick EH39 4PL
Tel 01620 892608
Web www.glebehouse-nb.co.uk

Kirknewton House

You get the best of two worlds at Kirknewton: a large, comfortable house in peaceful landscaped woodland gardens, and Edinburgh, 30 minutes by car or train. Rooms are lovely and large, there's a fine, polished oak staircase, fresh flowers in the hall, rugs on the floor; and lots of fruit for breakfast – feast in the stately dining room, or snug up to the Aga in the kitchen. Tinkie is a county organiser for Scotland's Gardens Scheme and knows all about private gardens in the area. In hers, find azaleas and rhododendrons in spring, primulas and meconopsis scattered throughout, and a herbaceous border in a walled garden – wonderful in summer.

Price	£100. Singles £50.
Rooms	2: 1 double, 1 four-poster, each with separate bath.
Meals	Dinner £25-£50 by advance arrangement only. Pub/restaurant 4 miles.
Closed	Christmas-February.
Directions	From either A70 or A71 take B7031. 0.25 miles from Kirknewton going south, drive on left opposite small cottage.

Tinkie & Charles Welwood
Kirknewton EH27 8DA

Tel 01506 881235
Web www.kirknewtonestate.co.uk

Blair Adam

If staying in a place with genuine Adam features is special, how much more so in the Adams' family home! They've been in this corner of Fife since 1733: John laid out the walled garden, son William was a prominent politician, Sir Walter Scott used to come and stay... you may be similarly inspired. The house stands in a swathe of parkland and forest overlooking the hills and Loch Leven, with big, friendly, light-flooded rooms filled with intriguing contents. The pretty bedroom is on the ground floor and you eat in the private dining room or with the family in the kitchen – you choose.

Price	From £90. Singles from £50.
Rooms	1 twin.
Meals	Dinner £20. Restaurants 5 miles.
Closed	December-January.
Directions	From M90 exit 5, B996 south for Kelty. Right for Maryburgh, through village, right through pillars onto drive, under m'way via tunnel; up to house.

Keith & Elizabeth Adam
Kelty KY4 0JF
Tel 01383 831221
Email adamofblairadam@hotmail.com

Ladywell House

Up the farm track to the large stone manse – once holiday home of Frances Shand Kydd. Duncan and Camilla invite you in to a big elegant hall and smart spotless bedrooms above, where cool neutrals mix with rich flashes of colour, crisp linen hugs squishy goose down, shutters open to wide views – and Diana's room stays largely untouched. In the drawing room are flamboyant curtains and huge cream sofas, an honesty tray and Camilla's clever jewellery for sale. Duncan cooks a locally sourced breakfast as generous as all the rest; for the evening there's Falkland, with its shops, cobbles and delicious places to dine.

Price	£60-£80. Singles from £45.
Rooms	3: 1 double, 1 twin; 1 twin with separate bath.
Meals	Pub 10-minute walk.
Closed	Rarely.
Directions	A92 north; 1st exit at 'New Inn' r'bout, signed Falkland. 2.5 miles just before village, farm road on left signed Ladywell House. Then 1st right through black gates.

Duncan & Camilla Heaton Armstrong
Falkland KY15 7DE
Tel 01337 858414
Web www.ladywellhousefife.co.uk

The Inn at Lathones

You don't have to be a golfer to love this inn, but St Andrews is five miles west and after shooting three under par into the wind, your body will thank you for organising a night of luxury to follow. The inn goes back to 1603 – find stone walls, timber frames, painted panelling and a wood-burner in the sitting room. In the new extension are stylish suites with balconies overlooking fields, sparkling bathrooms and bedrooms laden with technological excess. But best of all is the food. Nick does 'trilogy' cooking – each course offers three micro-courses built around a central theme – good fun and preparation for golf the next day. *Minimum stay two nights at weekends.*

Price	£180-£245. Suites £295.
Rooms	21: 19 twins/doubles, 2 suites.
Meals	Lunch £14.50-£17.40. Dinner, à la carte, about £40. Packed lunch from £12.
Closed	Christmas & 2 weeks in January.
Directions	From Kirkcaldy, or St Andrews, A915 to Largoward. Inn 1 mile north on roadside.

Nick White
Lathones, St Andrews KY9 1JE

Tel 01334 840494
Web www.theinn.co.uk

Kinkell

An avenue of beech trees patrolled by guinea fowl leads to the house. If the sea views and the salty smack of St Andrews Bay air don't get you, step inside and have your senses tickled. The elegant drawing room has two open fires, rosy sofas, a grand piano – gorgeous. Bedrooms and bathrooms are immaculate, sunny and warm. There's great cooking too; Sandy and Frippy excel in the kitchen and make full use of local produce. From the front door head down to the beach, walk the wild coast, jump on a quad bike, try your hand at clay pigeon shooting. All this and wonderful hosts.

Price	£80. Singles from £50.
Rooms	3 twins/doubles.
Meals	Dinner £25. Restaurants in St Andrews, 2 miles.
Closed	Rarely.
Directions	From St Andrews, A917 for 2 miles for Crail. Driveway in 1st line of trees on left after St Andrews.

Sandy & Frippy Fyfe
St Andrews KY16 8PN
Tel 01334 472003
Web www.kinkell.com

Falside Smiddy

The old smithy sits right on a bend (peaceful at night) but city dwellers won't mind. Saved from dereliction by Rosie and musical, chatty Keith, it is a home you are invited to share. Expect fresh flowers, maps on walls, books, boots and interesting ephemera – not for style seekers but this place is interesting and different. Small rooms have homemade biscuits and hat stands for clothes, bath and shower rooms are spotlessly clean. Rosie cooks a truly good breakfast and turns berries into jams, and the wood-burner makes winters cosy. Lovely walks from the door to the sea and you are close to golf courses.

Price	£56-£65. Singles £40.
Rooms	2 twins.
Meals	Pub 2 miles. St Andrews 4 miles.
Closed	Occasionally.
Directions	From St Andrews, A917 for Crail. After 4 miles, ignore turning for Boarhills, & continue to small river. Over bridge; house 2nd on left.

Rosie & Keith Birkinshaw
Boarhills, St Andrews KY16 8PT

Tel 01334 880479
Email rosiebirk@btinternet.com

Cambo House

This is a Victorian mansion in the grand style, with staff. Bedrooms are magnificent; the 'Yellow' room was once used for servicing the dining room (which is almost a banqueting hall). Breakfast here in the summer with views of Lady Erskine's garden, retire to a delightful guest sitting room that overlooks a fountain. If you B&B in the studio apartment, with its little sitting area in a turret, you may come and go as you please. As for the gardens, they are stunning all year: a lilac walk through 26 varieties, 70 acres of woodland following a burn to the sea, a two-acre walled garden and a brilliant potager; always something new here and buzzing with success.

Price	£90-£130. Singles £47-£65.
Rooms	3 + 2: 2 four-posters (1 with separate bath/shower); 1 twin/double (let in conjunction with four-poster). 2 B&B or self-catering studios, each for 2.
Meals	Dinner from £45. Pub 1 mile.
Closed	Christmas & New Year.
Directions	A917 to Crail, through Kingsbarns. Follow signs for Cambo Gardens, follow drive to house.

Sir Peter & Lady Erskine
Kingsbarns, St Andrews KY16 8QD
Tel 01333 450054
Web www.camboestate.com

18 Queen's Terrace

So peaceful that it's hard to imagine that you're in the heart of St Andrews and a mere ten-minute walk from the Royal & Ancient golf club. Jill's stylish and traditional home shows off her artistic flair; the light, restful drawing room and elegant dining room are full of character, sunlight and flowers. Large bedrooms have especially comfortable beds, crisp linens, whisky and water, and poetry and prose on bedside tables. An enchanting place – and Jill, friendly and generous, is a mine of information on art, gardens and walks; sit on the terrace in summer and admire the water garden. *Children over 12 welcome.*

Price	From £85. Singles £65-£70.
Rooms	4: 3 doubles, 1 twin.
Meals	Dinner, 3 courses with wine, £20-£35.
Closed	Rarely.
Directions	Into St Andrews on A917; pass Old Course Hotel. Right at 2nd mini r'bout, left through arch at 2nd mini r'bout. 250 yds, right into Queens Gardens. Right at T-junc. On left opp. church.

Jill Hardie
St Andrews KY16 9QF

Tel 01334 478849
Web www.18queensterrace.com

Fincraigs

Immersed in delightful, forgotten countryside, this 18th-century farmhouse, once the factor's house, has an air of great comfort and warmth; Felicity and Tom make you feel instantly at home. There's a sunny drawing room with open fire and old family pieces, and a guest sitting area upstairs. Two pretty bedrooms have lovely linen and fine views over the garden and rolling hills. Fincraigs' ten acres, presided over by roaming hens and ducks, include an orchard and walled garden; expect fabulous home cooking and Tom's delicious wines. Fishing villages, the Tay estuary, East Neuk, Dundee and St Andrews are close by.

Price	From £80. Singles from £40.
Rooms	2: 1 double; 1 twin with separate bath.
Meals	Dinner, 3 courses, from £25. Pubs 3-5 miles.
Closed	Occasionally.
Directions	From A92 heading north, left after Rathillet, at Balmerino/Gauldry sign. Fincraigs 1 mile from main road on left.

Felicity & Tom Gilbey
Kilmany, Cupar KY15 4QQ
Tel 01382 330256
Web www.fincraigs.com

The Old Ferryman's House

This former ferryman's house is small, homely and delightful, and just yards from the river Spey with its spectacular mountain views. Explore the countryside or relax in the garden with a tray of tea and homemade treats; there are plants tumbling from whisky barrels and baskets. The sitting room is cosy with a wood-burning stove and lots of books (no TV). Generous Elizabeth, a keen traveller who lived in the Sudan, cooks delicious and imaginative meals: wild salmon, herbs from the garden, heathery honeycomb, homemade bread and preserves. An unmatched spot for explorers, and very good value.

Price	£55. Singles £27.50.
Rooms	3: 1 double, 1 twin, 1 single, sharing 1 bath & 2 wcs.
Meals	Dinner, 3 courses, £19.50. BYO. Packed lunch £6.
Closed	Occasionally in winter.
Directions	From A9, follow main road markings through village, pass golf club & cross river. From B970 to Boat of Garten; house on left, just before river.

Elizabeth Matthews
Boat of Garten PH24 3BY
Tel 01479 831370

Invergloy House

A peaceful, no-smoking home run by Margaret, a professional musician and James, a retired chemical engineer. It is a converted coach house with stables in the beautiful Great Glen and sits in 50 wild lochside acres of rhododendron, woodland and wonderful trees. Bedrooms are traditional, warm and welcoming; views of Loch Lochy and the mountains from the big picture window in the guest drawing room are spectacular. Walk to the private shingle beach on the loch, spot the wild roe deer in the grounds, savour the secluded peace and quiet. *Children over eight welcome.*

Price	From £72. Singles £46.
Rooms	2: 1 double, 1 twin.
Meals	Restaurants 2-5 miles.
Closed	Christmas & New Year.
Directions	From Spean Bridge north on A82. After 5 miles, house signed on left.

Margaret & James Cairns
Spean Bridge PH34 4DY

Tel 01397 712681
Web www.invergloy-house.co.uk

Tomdoun Hotel

A quirky little place wrapped up in the middle of nowhere: in good weather Reception moves onto the veranda and the dogs sunbathe on lilos. Interiors are stylishly unpretentious (posh, but old!), there's a country-house dining room for breakfasts, and a smouldering coal fire in the lively bar. Come to fish – the hotel has rights on the loch and river below; if you're lucky, they'll cook your catch for supper. Bedrooms are simple, homely, nicely priced, full of colour; those at the front have huge Glengarry views. There's loads to do: clay-pigeon shooting, white-water rafting, waterskiing, abseiling, mountain biking, and 35 munros to climb.

Price	£80-£110. Singles from £35.
Rooms	10: 3 doubles, 2 family, all en suite; 3 doubles, 1 twin, 1 single all sharing 2 baths.
Meals	Packed lunch £7.95. Bar meals from £9.95. Dinner, 3 courses, from £18.95.
Closed	Never.
Directions	A82 north from Fort William, then A87 west from Invergarry. After 5 miles, left for Glengarry. Hotel 6 miles up on right.

Michael Pearson
Glengarry, Invergarry PH35 4HS

Tel 01809 511218
Web www.tomdoun.com

Loch Ness Lodge

A super-smart country house built from scratch in 2006 and overlooking the famous loch. There are oak floors, period colours, designer fabrics and fresh flowers, an open fire in the airy sitting room, red Zoffany wallpaper in the restaurant. Bedrooms are seriously indulging with huge beds and extravagant bathrooms. One is a riot of red crushed velvet, another has armchairs in a turret. Five have sublime loch views, all have bathrobes, CD players and flat-screen TVs. Expect a sauna, hot tub and treatment room, too, and dinners that are five-course feasts. Both coasts are equally accessible, and don't miss Glen Affric, one of Scotland's loveliest.

Price	£180-£230. Suites £280. Cottages £560-£930 per week.
Rooms	7 + 5: 3 twins/doubles, 2 doubles, 2 suites. 5 self-catering cottages (3 for 2, 2 for 4).
Meals	Dinner, 5 courses, £45. Lunch by arrangement.
Closed	3 January-end February.
Directions	A82 south from Inverness for 10 miles. On right after Clansman Hotel.

Scott Sutherland
Brachla, Loch Ness-side, Inverness IV3 8LA
Tel 01456 459469
Web www.lodgeatlochness.co.uk

Cawdor Cottages, Cawdor Estate

Limpid salmon pools, ragged moorland, sweet heather, a fairytale castle, an estate steeped in history. The family have been here for 700 years, the first Thane making a rebellious appearance in *Macbeth*. The traditional estate cottages (scattered about pebble-banked rivers and in plunging glens) are havens of sophisticated elegance. All have log fires, free-standing baths, antique brass beds; wine and a welcome hamper greet every guest. There's fishing on the local loch, and each cottage has descriptions of beautiful local walks and contact details for a local alternative therapist if the unimagineable happens – you can't unwind!

Price	£480-£1,070 per week. Please call for details.
Rooms	Achneim for 2. Lochanshelloch for 6.
Meals	Pub walking distance.
Closed	Never.
Directions	Directions given on booking.

Carol Cooper
Cawdor, Nairn, Inverness IV12 5RE

Tel 01667 402402
Web www.cawdor.com

Craigiewood

The best of both worlds: the remoteness of the Highlands (red kites, wild goats) and Inverness just four miles. The landscape surrounding this elegant cottage exudes a sense of ancient mystery augmented by these six acres – home to woodpeckers, roe deer and glorious roses. Inside, maps, walking sticks, two cats and a lovely, family-home feel – what you'd expect from delightful owners. Bedrooms, old-fashioned and cosy, overlook a garden reclaimed from Black Isle gorse. Gavin runs garden tours and can take you off to Inverewe, Attadale, Cawdor and Dunrobin Castle. Warm, peaceful, special.

Price	£70-£80. Singles £40.
Rooms	2 twins.
Meals	Pub 2 miles.
Closed	Christmas & New Year.
Directions	A9 north over Kessock Bridge. At N. Kessock junc. filter left to r'bout to Kilmuir. After 0.25 miles, right to Kilmuir; follow road uphill, left at top, then straight on. Ignore 'No Through Road' sign, pass Drynie Farm, follow road to right; house 1st left.

Araminta & Gavin Dallmeyer
North Kessock, Inverness IV1 3XG

Tel 01463 731628
Web www.craigiewood.co.uk

Assynt House

So impressive is this 18th-century dower house that the Roosevelts spent some of their honeymoon here; a century on, trees were growing through the roof. Undeterred, the new owners began a five-year restoration: wood-panelling, comfy sofas, logs, candles, flowers – a super-relaxed place to stay. Bedrooms are big and stylish with fabulous king-size beds; climb a spiral staircase to a room with a telescope and views of Cromarty Firth. Bathrooms are, without exception, stunning; and the light, beautifully equipped kitchen is perfect for drinking and chilling. Outside are acres of wooded hills, soaring eagles and a bothy where your friendly hosts live. Superb.

Price	£3,100 per week (£4,000 at Christmas & New Year).
Rooms	House for 14 (18 with cots & fold-away beds): 3 doubles; 4 twin/doubles.
Meals	Dinner £35-£40 per person.
Closed	Rarely.
Directions	Directions given on booking.

Graham & Elizabeth Waugh
Evanton IV16 9XW
Tel 01349 832923
Web www.assynthouse.com

Wemyss House

The peace is palpable, the setting overlooking the Cromarty Firth is stunning. Take an early morning stroll and spot buzzards, pheasants, rabbits and roe deer. The deceptively spacious house with sweeping maple floors is flooded with light and fabulous views, big bedrooms are warmly decorated with Highland rugs and tweeds, there's Christine's grand piano in the living room, Stuart's handcrafted furniture at every turn, and a sweet rescue dog called Bella. Aga breakfasts include homemade bread, preserves and eggs from happy hens. Dinners are delicious, Christine and Stuart are wonderful hosts and readers are full of praise.

Price	From £80.
Rooms	3: 2 doubles, 1 twin.
Meals	Dinner, 4 courses, £30. Restaurants 15-minute drive.
Closed	Rarely.
Directions	From Inverness, A9 north. At Nigg r'bout, right onto B9175. Through Arabella; left at sign to Hilton & Shandwick; right towards Nigg; past church; 1 mile, right onto private road. House on right.

Christine Asher & Stuart Clifford
Bayfield, Tain IV19 1QW

Tel 01862 851212
Web www.wemysshouse.com

Glenmorangie, The Highland Home at Cadboll

Glenmorangie – glen of tranquillity. And so it is; this is heaven. Owned by the eponymous distillery, this 1700s farmhouse of thick walls and immaculate interiors stands in glorious country, with a tree-lined path to the beach. Bedrooms are exceptional and flood with light: you get decanters of whisky, *fleur de lys* wallpaper, tartan blankets and country views. Downstairs, the portrait of the Sheriff of Cromarty hangs on the wall, a fire crackles between plump sofas in the drawing room, and views of the garden draw you out. A real find, with levels of service to surpass most others. All this, and golf at Royal Dornoch, Tain and Brora.

Price	Half-board £165-£195 p.p.
Rooms	9: 6 twins/doubles, 3 cottage suites.
Meals	Half-board only. Light lunch from £7. Dinner for non-residents, £45.
Closed	3-23 January.
Directions	A9 north from Inverness for 33 miles to Nigg r'bout. Right on B9175, for Nigg, over r'way crossing for 1.5 miles, then left, following signs.

Martin Baxter
Fearn, Tain IV20 1XP

Tel 01862 871671
Web www.theglenmorangiehouse.com

Loch Eye House

A serene place for walkers, golfers, naturalists – and anyone who enjoys sociable dinner at an elegant table where mahogany gleams and wine glasses sparkle. It was Lucinda's dream to live here – she has childhood memories of skating on the loch; now the handsome, sunny house (15th century at the back, 1870 at the front) is exquisitely furnished and filled with fresh flowers. Bedrooms have perfect proportions and harmonious colours, bathrooms are immaculate, one with loch views: spot rare birdlife as you soak. The lawns sweep towards the loch and every view is sublime.

Price	£90. Singles £45.
Rooms	3: 1 double; 1 double, 1 twin, sharing bath.
Meals	Dinner, 3 courses, £30.
Closed	Occasionally.
Directions	A9 for Tain, then B9165 for Fearn. 1st left for Loandhu, then 1.5 miles & on left.

Lucinda Poole
Fearn IV20 1RS

Tel 01862 832297
Email loofy@ndirect.co.uk

Linsidecroy

Heaven in the Highlands with stunning valley and mountain views. The house, built in 1863 was part of the Duke of Sutherland's estate; Robert, a factor, first set eyes on it 20 years ago and now it is home. A sublime renovation gives you walls of books, valley views and an open fire in the airy drawing room. Super bedrooms come with rugs, crisp linen, books galore and fresh flowers. There are two terraces, one for breakfast, one for pre-dinner drinks; all around you Davina's remarkable garden is taking shape. You can fish and walk, play some golf, or head north to Tongue through Britain's wildest land. Magical.

Price	£80. Singles £50.
Rooms	2: 1 double, 1 twin.
Meals	Hotel 6 miles.
Closed	Christmas, Easter & occasionally.
Directions	A836 west out of Bonar Bridge. After 4 miles, left onto A837. Cross Shin river, then right towards Rosehall & Lochinver, 1.5 miles, double wooden gates on right. House is 150 yds up drive.

Robert & Davina Howden
Invershin, Lairg IV27 4EU

Tel 01549 421255
Email howden@linsidecroy.wanadoo.co.uk

South & West Cottages

You're in the wilds of the far north with huge beauty all around: head off in any direction to find magical landscapes – the sands of Tongue, mountains and azure seas, monsters in lochs and great golf. These rose-clad estate cottages aren't grand but as warm and snug as you'd want them in a remote landscape and come clad from top to toe in raw pine, giving the feel of a big cabin. You get tartan curtains, neutral colours, books galore and fabulous views. Both have terraces, and while the road passes beyond, traffic is rare. Kitchens come fully equipped, comfy sofas lie on pretty rugs, country bedrooms are simply stylish. A brilliant escape.

Price	£225-£480 per week.
Rooms	South Cottage for 4. West Cottage for 2.
Meals	Hotel 6 miles.
Closed	Never.
Directions	A836 west out of Bonar Bridge. After 4 miles, left onto A837. Cross Shin river, then right towards Rosehall & Lochinver, 1.5 miles, double wooden gates on right. House is 150 yds up drive.

Robert & Davina Howden
Linsidecroy, Invershin, Lairg IV27 4EU
Tel 01549 421255
Web www.highlandcottages.org

St Callan's Manse

Fun, laughter and conversation flow in this warm, relaxed and happy home. You share it with prints, paintings, antiques, sofas and amazing memorabilia – and three dogs, nine ducks, 14 hens and 1,200 teddy bears of every shape, size and origin. Snug bedrooms have pretty fabrics, old armoires, sheepskin rugs, tartan blankets. Caroline cooks delicious breakfasts and dinners; Robert, a fund of knowledgeable anecdotes, can arrange just about anything. All this in incomparable surroundings: glens, forests, buzzards, deer and the odd golden eagle. A gem. *2.5% credit card charge. Dogs by arrangement.*

Price	£80. Singles £65.
Rooms	2: 1 double with separate bath; 1 double with separate shower.
Meals	Dinner, 2-4 courses, £14.50-£25. BYO. Pub/restaurant in village, 1.5 miles.
Closed	Occasionally.
Directions	A839 to Lairg. Cross small bridge in Rogart; sharp right uphill, for St Callan's church. House 1.5 miles on, on right, next to church.

Robert & Caroline Mills
Rogart IV28 3XE
Tel 01408 641363
Web www.miltonbankcottages.co.uk

Thrumster House

A Victorian laird's house in 12 acres of sycamore-wooded estate. Drive south a mile to the 5,000-year-old neolithic remains of the Yarrow Archeological Trail for brochs, round houses and long cairns, then back to the big old house, "steamboat gothic" in the words of an American guest. The vaulted hall gives an ecclesiastical feel, with fires burning at both ends and a grand piano on the landing (it gets played wonderfully). Big bedrooms have mahogany dressers, brass beds, floral wallpapers, lots of books. Islay and Catherine look after guests well and conversation flows. There's free trout fishing too.

Price	£80. Singles £45.
Rooms	2: 1 double; 1 twin with separate bath.
Meals	Dinner, 3 courses with wine, £30.
Closed	Rarely.
Directions	A99 north through Ulbster. After 2 miles, pass church & 'Yarrow Archaeological Trail' sign, then 1st left (200 yds) & up drive to house.

Islay MacLeod
Thrumster KW1 5TX
Tel 01955 651387
Web www.thrumster.co.uk

Mackay's Rooms

This is the north-west tip of Scotland and it's magnificent: huge skies, sandy beaches, aquamarine seas, cliffs and caves – and you'll have it mostly to yourself. Mackay's is the only place to stay in town, its jaunty contemporary colours mixing with stone walls and stripped floors to great effect. Bedrooms are extremely comfy – big wooden beds, crisp white linen – and bathrooms are excellent. Breakfast sets you up for the day – whisky porridge, venison sausages – so head east to the beach at Ceannabeinne, west for cliff-top golf, or catch a ferry to Cape Wrath and scan for whales. If you like big, remote landscapes, you'll love it here.

Price	£100-£130. Singles from £90. Cottage £500-£950 per week.
Rooms	7 + 1: 5 doubles, 2 twins. 1 self-catering cottage for 6.
Meals	Lunch from £5. Dinner, 3 courses, £25-£30.
Closed	November-Easter.
Directions	A838 north from Rhiconich. After 19 miles enter Durness village. Mackay's is on right-hand side opposite memorial.

Fiona Mackay
Durness IV27 4PN

Tel 01971 511202
Web www.visitmackays.com

The Albannach

It may take a while to get here, but you won't regret it. The glimmering seas, rugged mountains and empty roads are a tonic for the soul. Colin and Lesley's faultless food is worth the trip alone, but the interior is no less alluring; fat white sofas in the conservatory, a fire in the panelled snug, and cherry red walls in the baronial dining room. Bedrooms are big or bigger, all dressed in Sunday-best fabrics with Farrow & Ball colours, carafes of water and Bose sound systems. The suites are majestic with unbeatable bathrooms, the simpler rooms are not simple at all; everything here is fantastic. Walk, fish, some people swim. Heaven.

Price	Half-board £125-£170 p.p. Singles £200. Winter weekend breaks available.
Rooms	5: 2 doubles, 3 suites.
Meals	Half-board only. Lunch, by arrangement, from £12. Dinner, 5 courses, £50 for non-residents.
Closed	January & February.
Directions	North from Ullapool on A835, then A837 for Lochinver. In village, left, over bridge, for Baddidarrach. House signed left after half a mile.

Colin Craig & Lesley Crosfield
Baddidaroch, Lochinver IV27 4LP
Tel 01571 844407
Web www.thealbannach.co.uk

The Torridon

Walkers pour off the hills to recover in luxury here – at the 1887 shooting lodge with 58 acres racing down to a loch. Mountains rise around you, red deer, sea eagles and otters pass through. Inside: a huge fire in the panelled hall, a zodiac ceiling in the plush drawing room, and 300 malts in the pitch pine bar. Bedrooms are a treat, some big, others bigger, all packed with spoiling extras. Some come smart contemporary, others are deliciously traditional. The two-acre vegetable garden is a work of art and provides much for the table, so feast on fresh food sublimely cooked. You're in the middle of nowhere, but you wouldn't be anywhere else.

Price	Half-board £132.50-£237.50 p.p. Boathouse from £750 per week.
Rooms	19 + 1: 10 doubles, 1 twin, 1 single, 2 four-posters, 5 suites. Self-catering boathouse for 4.
Meals	Half-board only (except boathouse). Lunch from £5. Dinner, 5 courses, £40 for non-residents.
Closed	January.
Directions	A9 to Inverness, A835 to Garve, A832 to Kinlochewe, A896 to Annat (not Torridon). In village, right by sea.

Daniel & Rohaise Rose-Bristow
Torridon, Achnasheen IV22 2EY

Tel 01445 791242
Web www.thetorridon.com

Tanglewood House

Down a steep drive through stunning landscape to this modern, curved house on the shore of Loch Broom – and distant views of the old fishing port of Ullapool. The drawing room is filled with antique rugs, fine fabrics, original paintings, flowers and a grand piano; bask in the views from the floor-to-ceiling window. Bedrooms are delightful: bold colours, crisp linen, proper bath tubs with fluffy towels. Anne gives you just-squeezed orange juice and eggs from her hens for breakfast, and delicious dinners; explore the wild garden then stroll to the rocky private beach for a swim in the loch. Superb. *Minimum stay two nights.*

Price	£88-£102. Singles £69-£76.
Rooms	3: 1 double, 2 twins.
Meals	Dinner, 4 courses, £36. BYO. Pubs in village 0.5 miles.
Closed	Christmas & New Year.
Directions	On outskirts of Ullapool from Inverness on A835, left immed. after 4th 40mph sign. Take cattle grid on right & left fork down to house.

Anne Holloway
Ullapool IV26 2TB
Tel 01854 612059
Web www.tanglewoodhouse.co.uk

Tigh an Eilean

Tigh an Eilean is the Holy Grail of the West Coast – a perfect place in every way, from its position by the sea in this very pretty village, to the magnificence of the Torridon mountains that rise around. Inside, smart country-house interiors are just the ticket, there are a couple of sitting rooms, an honesty bar and an award-winning restaurant that looks out to sea. Bedrooms (most have the view) come with colourful fabrics, crisp linen, fitted wardrobes, the odd antique. Delicious food flies from the kitchen and Shieldaig, a working fishing village, still gathers in the bar, to play its fiddles and sip the odd malt.

Price	£160. Singles from £75. Half-board from £115 p.p.
Rooms	11: 5 doubles, 3 twins, 3 singles.
Meals	Lunch & dinner in bar, £5-£25. Restaurant dinner £44. Packed lunches available.
Closed	November-March.
Directions	On loch front in centre of Shieldaig.

Christopher & Cathryn Field
Shieldaig, Loch Torridon IV54 8XN

Tel 01520 755251
Email tighaneilean@keme.co.uk

The Berry

Drive through miles of spectacular landscape then bask in the final approach down a winding single-track road to the hamlet of Allt-Na-Subh – just five houses by the stunning loch. Joan, who paints, is friendly and kind, and her Rayburn-warmed kitchen the hub of this croft-style modern house. Inside is fresh and light with simple bedrooms – one up, one down; the sitting room has open fires and south-facing views. Eat fish straight from the boats, stride the hills and spot golden eagles, red deer and otters. The perfect place for naturalists and artists, or those seeking solace. *Skye is a 20-minute drive.*

Price	£60. Singles from £30.
Rooms	2: 1 double with separate shower; 1 double sharing bath.
Meals	Dinner, 3 courses with wine, £28. Packed lunch £7. Pub 20-minute drive.
Closed	Rarely.
Directions	From A87 at Dornie follow signs for Killilin, Conchra & Salachy. House 2.7 miles on left.

Joan Ashburner
Allt-Na-Subh, Dornie, Kyle of Lochalsh
IV40 8DZ
Tel 01599 588259

Tigh An Dochais

A contemporary, award-winning, 'see-through' house on a narrow strip of land between the road and the rocky shoreline, with stunning views across Broadford bay and the mountains beyond. Full-length windows and a cathedral ceiling allow light to flood in to an oak-floored sitting room with a wood-burner and super modern art. Downstairs are bedrooms with crisp white linen, tartan throws and modern bathrooms with underfloor heating. Neil is passionate about local food; try black pudding from Stornoway at breakfast, good fish and game for supper. Step straight onto the beach here, or stride out for the hills.

Price	£70-£80. Singles £55-£65.
Rooms	3: 2 doubles, 1 twin/double.
Meals	Dinner, 4 courses, £22-£25. BYO. Packed lunch £5. Pub/restaurant 200 yds.
Closed	Rarely.
Directions	Leave Skye Bridge & follow A87 to Broadford. After 6 miles pass Hebridean Hotel on left, house is 200 yds further up A87 on right.

Neil Hope
13 Harrapool, Isle of Skye IV49 9AQ

Tel	01471 820022
Web	www.skyebedbreakfast.co.uk

Viewfield House

This old ancestral pile stands above Portree Bay with views tumbling down to the Sound of Rassay. Twenty acres of gardens wrap around you, with croquet on the lawn. Expect some aristocratic touches: hunting trophies, a grand piano, family oils, wood carvings from distant lands, a flurry of antiques – all of which blend grandeur with humour. Bedrooms are big, some vast, all come in country-house style with traditional fabrics, well-laundered sheets and sea views from those at the front. Dive into Skye – wildlife, mountains, sea lochs and castles await. Light suppers are on tap – salads, salmon, spotted dick; alternatively, dine out on Skye's natural larder.

Price	£80-£130. Singles £40-£65.
Rooms	12: 4 doubles, 3 twins/doubles, 2 twins, 2 singles all en suite. 1 double with separate bath.
Meals	Light supper £3-£14. Packed lunch £5.40.
Closed	Mid-October-Easter.
Directions	On A87, coming from south, driveway entrance on left just before the Portree National filling station.

Hugh Macdonald
Portree, Isle of Skye IV51 9EU

Tel 01478 612217
Web www.viewfieldhouse.com

Greshornish House Hotel

A sheep-straddled road peters out at this supremely peaceful hotel, in acres of woodland gardens with views across Loch Greshornish to the Totternish peninsular. Inside, a slightly eccentric country house; Neil and Rosemary are everywhere and run it with infectious charm. Downstairs, a fire glows in the half-panelled sitting room, afternoon tea is in the conservatory and splendid local food is served in the dining room. Bedrooms are mostly large and come in a warm traditional style; all have excellent views of the water or gardens. Outside is croquet, a terrace for drinks and paths to the loch; porpoises, seals or otters all come through.

Price	£110-£198.
Rooms	9: 4 doubles, 2 twins/doubles, 1 twin, 2 family.
Meals	Lunch £5.50-£22.50. Dinner, 3 courses, about £38. Packed lunch about £6.
Closed	Christmas. Occasionally in winter.
Directions	A87 through Portree then west on A850 for Dunvegan. Signed right after 10 miles. 2.5 miles down single track road to hotel.

Neil & Rosemary Colquhoun
Portree, Isle of Skye IV51 9PN

Tel 01470 582266
Web www.greshornishhouse.com

Lyndale Gate Lodge, Lyndale House

The sky envelops you, sea, lochs and views of distant isles surround you, and a little burn runs in front of your 'inkpot-style' cottage sitting inside woodland. Inside, all is immensely comfortable and gently stylish. The living room is open plan, there's a fresh little double bedroom downstairs and a twin up, with beds set end to end; the bathroom is blue-panelled, white-walled, sparkling. Wander down the wooded driveway to the shore: spot seals, fish, or explore Skye on a pony. Just enjoy the sunsets and absolute peace.

Price	£375-£850 per week.
Rooms	Lodge for 4 (1 double; 1 twin).
Meals	Pub 3 miles.
Closed	Never.
Directions	Directions given on booking.

Marcus & Linda Ridsdill Smith
Edinbane, Isle of Skye IV51 9PX

Tel 01470 582329
Web www.lyndale.net

Laundry Cottage & Stables Cottage, Lyndale House

At the bottom of the garden, views stretch across the loch towards the Outer Hebrides, the sea laps the shore and the sunsets and space live long in the memory. Two cottages, tucked away in stillness on a private estate, surrounded by happy hens and towering trees, will charm you: good beds and furniture, big sofas, interesting art (some by Linda), gowns on the backs of bedroom doors, heating that warms the Caithness stone floors. Marcus has created a biodynamic kitchen garden and an organic holding, and he won't mind if you lounge in a corner of his cruciform-walled garden.

Price	£350-£650 per week.
Rooms	Laundry Cottage & Stables Cottage, both for 2.
Meals	Pub 3 miles.
Closed	Never.
Directions	Directions given on booking.

Marcus & Linda Ridsdill Smith
Edinbane, Isle of Skye IV51 9PX
Tel 01470 582329
Web www.lyndale.net

Stein Inn

A small inn down by the water where Angus cooks super fresh food and refuses to put up his prices. You're bang on the loch on a road that goes nowhere. The islands sparkle in the distance, fishermen land their catch on the jetty, sunsets streak the sky red. Inside, stone walls, smouldering fires, pine cladding and a bustling bar that's crammed with locals at weekends. Bedrooms above (some big, some small) fit the bill perfectly. They're spotless, colourful, comfy, with a warm country style and an honest price. Corncrakes and sea eagles pass through, the northern lights sparkle in winter. The position is perfect, Skye at its loveliest.

Price	£60-£90. Singles £35-£50.
Rooms	5: 2 doubles, 2 family, 1 single.
Meals	Lunch & dinner £3-£20.
Closed	Christmas Day & New Year's Day.
Directions	From Isle of Skye bridge, A850 to Portree. Follow sign to Uig for 4 miles, left on A850 for Dunvegan for 14 miles. Hard right turn to Waternish on B886. Stein 4.5 miles along loch side.

Angus & Teresa McGhie
Stein, Waternish, Isle of Skye IV55 8GA

Tel	01470 592362
Web	www.stein-inn.co.uk

The Old Byre

A fab spot on the Waternish peninsula: spot whales, otters, seals and basking sharks. Lap it all up from your stone cowshed studio, simple on the outside, contemporary within. An open-plan living area focuses on a wood-burning stove; double-glazed patio doors pull light and views in – and keep raging gales out. You sleep on a supremely comfortable sofabed downstairs and relax on a sofa on the mezzanine, beneath which is a slate shower room with luscious soaps and soft towels. Local materials and craftsmen were used for almost everything – and the village guards a fantastic community of artists, potters, fishermen, and the oldest pub on Skye.

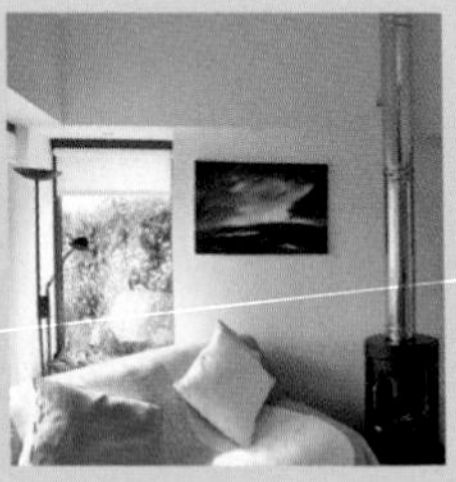

Price	£450 per week.
Rooms	Studio for 2 (1 sofabed).
Meals	Inn & restaurant 5-minute walk.
Closed	November-March.
Directions	Directions given on booking.

Elma Sands
Waternish, Isle of Skye IV55 8GD
Tel 01470 592332
Web www.ternhouse.com

Ullinish Country Lodge

A sparkling whitewashed Georgian farmhouse under a vast sky; views stretch across Loch Harport to the Talisker distillery. Samuel Johnson stayed on his tour, though you can bet he didn't eat as well as you will here. Pam and Brian came to add to Skye's gastronomic reputation and have done just that: the food is fabulous. A total refurbishment reveals warm interiors: tartan carpets, leather sofas by the fire, a telescope for star gazing, plush bedrooms with big mahogany beds, silky crowns and watery views. Dolphins and whales pass, sea eagles patrol the skies. Head to the tidal island of Oronsay, discover standing stones and iron age remains.

Price	£120-£160. Singles from £90. Half-board from £135 p.p.
Rooms	6 doubles.
Meals	Light lunch from £12.90. Sunday lunch £16.95. Dinner, 4 courses, £45.
Closed	January & 1 week in November.
Directions	North from Skye bridge on A87, then A863 for Dunvegan. Thro' Bracadale and Struan signed left. House on right after 1 mile.

Brian & Pam Howard
Struan, Isle of Skye IV56 8FD
Tel 01470 572214
Web www.theisleofskye.co.uk

Doune

Arrive by boat (there's no road in): a ferry to Knoydart, one of the last great wildernesses. Find mountains, sea and beach – a wonderland of boundless peace. Martin and Jane look after you with unpretentious generosity, their dining room is the hub, pine-clad from top-to-toe with a stove to keep you warm and guitars for the odd ceilidh. Food is delicious – crab from the bay, lamb from the hill, homemade ice cream. Pine bedrooms along the veranda are as simple as they should be, with bunk galleries for children, and an open-plan lodge for groups. The walking is magnificent, the sunsets are breathtaking. *Boat pick-up Tuesday & Saturday: minimum stay three nights.*

Price	Full-board £72 p.p. per night or £432 p.p. per week. Lodge: full-board from £55 p.p. or £330 p.p. per week. Discounts for children.
Rooms	4 + 1: 2 doubles, 1 twin (with mezzanine beds for children), 1 single. Catered lodge for 12.
Meals	Full-board (includes packed lunch).
Closed	October-Easter.
Directions	Park in Mallaig; the boat will collect you at an agreed time.

Martin & Jane Davies
Knoydart, Mallaig PH41 4PL
Tel 01687 462667
Web www.doune-knoydart.co.uk

Kilcamb Lodge

A stupendous setting, with Loch Sunart at the end of the garden and Glas Bheinn rising beyond. As for Kilcamb, it has all the ingredients of the perfect country house with a touch of shipwreck chic: a smart yellow drawing room with a roaring fire, a ship's bell in the bar, super-comfy bedrooms that don't stint on colour, and a dining room that's won just about every award going. There's a 12-acre garden with half a mile of shore, so look for dolphins, otters and seals (and, if you're lucky, eagles). Ardnamurchan Point, the most westerly point in mainland Britain, is up the road and worth a visit. *Minimum stay two nights at weekends in May.*

Price	£130-£180. Suites £230. Singles from £95.
Rooms	10: 7 doubles, 3 suites.
Meals	Lunch from £7.50. Dinner, 4 courses, £48.
Closed	January. Limited opening November & February.
Directions	From Fort William, A82 south for 10 miles to Corran ferry, then A861 to Strontian. Hotel west of village on left, signed. A830 & A861 from Fort William takes an hour longer.

David & Sally Ruthven-Fox
Strontian PH36 4HY

Tel 01967 402257
Web www.kilcamblodge.co.uk

The Grange

A Victorian townhouse with its toes in the country: the mountain hovers above, the loch shimmers below and whales have been sighted from the breakfast table. Bedrooms, one in a turret, another with a terrace, are large, luscious, warm and inviting – all crushed velvet, beautiful blankets and immaculate linen. Bathrooms are breathtaking and ooze panache. Expect neutral colours, decanters of sherry, a carved wooden fireplace, a Louis XV bed. Thoughtful breakfasts are served at glass-topped tables with flowers and white china; Joan's warm vivacity and love of B&B makes her a wonderful hostess. *Self-catering byre for two also available, call for details.*

Price	£98-£110. Singles 10% off room rate.
Rooms	3 doubles.
Meals	Restaurants 12-minute walk.
Closed	Mid-November to Easter.
Directions	A82 Glasgow-Fort William; there, right up Ashburn Lane, next to Ashburn guesthouse. On left at top.

Joan & John Campbell
Grange Road, Fort William PH33 6JF
Tel 01397 705516
Web www.thegrange-scotland.co.uk

The Colonsay

Another fabulous Hebridean island, a perfect place to do nothing at all. Wander at will and find wild flowers in the machair, a golf course tended by sheep and huge sandy beaches across which cows roam. This is a splendid island base with an easy style – airy interiors, stripped floors, fires everywhere, friendly staff. There's a locals' bar for a pint (and a brewery on the island), a pretty sitting room, a dining room for super food and a decked terrace for drinks in the sun. Recently refurbished bedrooms have local art, warm colours, lovely fabrics and the best beds; those at the front have sea views, all have neat little bathrooms. Wonderful.

Price	£95-£145. Singles from £60.
Rooms	9: 4 doubles, 3 twins, 1 single, 1 family.
Meals	Lunch from £4.50. Packed lunch £7. Bar meals from £7.50. Dinner, 3 courses, about £25.
Closed	November & February.
Directions	Calmac ferries from Oban or Kennacraig (not Tue or Sat) or Highland Airways (Tue and Thur). Hotel on right, half a mile up road from jetty.

Scott & Becky Omar
Scalasaig PA61 7YP

Tel 01951 200316
Web www.thecolonsay.com

Minmore House

In 1822 George IV tasted Glenlivet whisky for the first time and it swiftly became his favourite tipple. Minmore was built four years later by George Smith, whose whisky the king so admired. These days there are over 100 malts to boggle the mind; plus roaring fires, comfy sofas, terraced gardens, jolly Jack Russells. Bedrooms span the scale, some cosy, others lavish; all have crisp linen, bathrobes and a drop of whisky. Windows frame views of the Ladder hills but it's Victor's cooking that holds your attention: hand-dived scallops, rack of Highland lamb, apple and calvados soufflé. Highland safaris can be arranged. *Minimum stay two nights weekends in summer.*

Price	£110-£152. Suites £162-£204. Singles from £70. Half-board from £96 p.p.
Rooms	9: 3 doubles, 4 twins, 2 suites.
Meals	Light lunch £15. Dinner, 4 courses, £41. Full picnic £15.
Closed	26 November-28 December.
Directions	From Aviemore, A95 north to Bridge of Avon; south on B9008 to Glenlivet. At top of hill, 400 yds before distillery.

Victor & Lynne Janssen
Glenlivet AB37 9DB

Tel	01807 590378
Web	www.minmorehousehotel.com

The Pines

Spin through the gate and meet the locals: roe deer, woodpeckers and red squirrels. This is a cosseting place and Gwen and Michael make you feel immediately at home. Inside: a conservatory with garden views, smart tables in the dining room (expect delicious food and menus discussed in advance), and a first-floor drawing room where big sofas wait in front of the fire and beautiful art crams the walls. Bedrooms have a traditional country style: sheets and blankets, fresh flowers, polished wood and bowls of fruit. Circular walks are easy to follow; if you keep going for a mile or two, you'll come to the banks of the beautiful Spey.

Price	£130. Singles £65. Half-board £100 p.p.
Rooms	5: 4 twins/doubles, 1 double.
Meals	Dinner, 4 courses, £34. Packed lunch available.
Closed	Mid-October-mid-March.
Directions	A95 north to Grantown. Right in town at 1st traffic lights on A939 for Tomintoul, 1st right into Woodside Ave. 500 yds on left.

Michael & Gwen Stewart
Woodside Avenue, Grantown-on-Spey
PH26 3JR
Tel 01479 872092
Web www.thepinesgrantown.co.uk

Inverugie

A handsome Georgian house with lofty porticos, generous bays, tall windows and impressive drive. The feel is solid and traditional inside: velvet sofas in sage-green and rose, floral curtains at pelmetted windows, touches of Art Deco... toile de Jouy in the double, cream padded headboards and new beds in the twin. The large dining and drawing rooms look over ancient woodland, pasture land and grazing sheep; beyond, beaches, castles, standing stones and rivers rich with salmon and trout. Lucy is a dynamo – finding time for riding, fieldsports, three young children and you; she even grinds her own flour for your bread.

Price	£60-£70.
Rooms	2: 1 twin/double; 1 double with separate bath.
Meals	Dinner £25. Pub 8 miles.
Closed	Christmas & New Year.
Directions	To Forres on A96, through Kinloss on B9089 to College of Roseisle village & over B9013. Veer right (for Duffus) & 1.3 miles on, left to Keam Farm. Past farm, house at end of road through stone pillars.

Lucy Mackenzie
Hopeman IV30 5YB

Tel 01343 830253
Web www.inverugiehouse.co.uk

Westfield House

Sweep up the drive to the grand home of an illustrious family: Macleans have lived here since 1862. Inside: polished furniture and burnished antiques, a tartan-carpeted hall, an oak stair hung with ancestral oils. John farms 500 acres while Veronica cooks sublimely; dinner is served at a long candelabra'd table, with vegetables from the vegetable garden. A winter fire crackles in the guest sitting room, old-fashioned bedrooms are warm and inviting (plump pillows, fine linen, books, lovely views), the peace is deep. A historic house in a perfect setting, run by the most charming people.

Price	£80. Singles from £40.
Rooms	3: 1 twin; 1 twin with separate bath & shower; 1 single with separate bath.
Meals	Dinner, 3 courses, £25. Pub 3 miles.
Closed	Rarely.
Directions	From Elgin, A96 west for Forres & Inverness; after 2.5 miles, right onto B9013 for Burghead; after 1 mile, signed right at x-roads. Cont. to 'Westfield House & Office'.

John & Veronica Maclean
Elgin IV30 8XL
Tel 01343 547308
Email veronicamaclean@hotmail.com

Blervie

The Meiklejohn coat of arms flies from the flagpole, an apple's throw from the orchard in which King Malcolm met his death. Blervie is a small 1776 mansion, "a restoration in progress", its finely proportioned rooms crammed with fresh flowers and splendid things to catch the eye. A large dresser swamped in china, a piano in the hall, books everywhere and the sweet smell of burnt beech from grand marble fireplaces. Big bedrooms have comfy old sofas at the feet of four-posters; bathrooms are eccentrically old-fashioned. Fiona and Paddy enjoy country pursuits and like to dine with their guests.

Price	£80.
Rooms	2: 1 four-poster; 1 four-poster with separate bath. Extra single bed.
Meals	Dinner, 4 courses, £28.
Closed	Christmas & New Year.
Directions	From A96 to Forres. South at clocktower, straight across r'bout onto B9010. Pass hospital; 1 mile on, left at Mains of Blervie sign. Right at farm.

Paddy & Fiona Meiklejohn
Forres IV36 2RH

Tel 01309 672358
Email meiklejohn@btinternet.com

Woodwick House

This northern outpost stands 200 yards up from the sea, with views across the Sound of Gairsay to a small archipelago. Inside, you find an extraordinary little place, not fancy for a moment (three of the rooms share a bathroom) but the spirit here is second to none. Bedrooms are simple and spotless, there's a fire in the sitting room, big views from the sunroom, a small dining room for good home cooking, a music room for the occasional concert, a library for good books and a TV room stacked with videos in case it rains. James is the star, has no airs and graces, and your trip to these extraordinary islands will be richer because of him.

Price	£68-£110. Singles £34-£75.
Rooms	7: 3 doubles, 1 twin, all en suite; 1 double, 1 twin, 1 single, with basins, all sharing bathroom.
Meals	Dinner, 3 courses, £26. Packed lunch £7, by arrangement.
Closed	Rarely.
Directions	From Kirkwall, A965 to Finstown, then right onto A966 for Evie. After 7 miles, 1st right after turning for Tingwall ferry. Left down track to house.

James Bryan
Evie KW17 2PQ
Tel 01856 751330
Web www.woodwickhouse.co.uk

Grenich Steading

Perched above silvery Loch Tummel is Lindsay's award-winning renovation of a once derelict barn. Inside, blue-and-white Portuguese tiles, seagrass matting and a wood-burning stove. You get a kitchen, dining and sitting room so you can self-cater too (minimum one week). Gaze upon mountain-to-loch views, walk in the unspoilt glen or visit the theatre at Pitlochry. Lindsay loves nurturing both garden and guests; her two Scottish deerhounds are welcoming too. The sunsets are fabulous, and there's so much to do you'll barely be inside. *Children over eight welcome. Minimum stay two nights weekends May-October.*

Price	£80. Singles £60. Self-catering £500 per week.
Rooms	2: 1 double; 1 twin sharing bath & sitting room (2nd room let to same party only).
Meals	Dinner by arrangement, October to March only, £26 including wine. Pub 0.75 miles.
Closed	Christmas & New Year.
Directions	From Pitlochry A9 for Killiecrankie. Left on B8019 for T. Bridge. 0.75 miles after Loch Tummel Inn, right up forestry track for 0.5 miles. Signed.

Lindsay Morison
Strathtummel, Pitlochry PH16 5RT
Tel 01882 634332

Rose Cottage, Dunalastair Estate

Rose Cottage stands in a secluded garden crammed with colourful shrubs, and you don't have to stray far for views of lochs and the Schiehallion Mountain. It's cheerfully decorated inside – perfect for dogs, wet wellies and little ones. There's a Rayburn in the kitchen, and shortbread, milk and garden flowers to welcome you. The sitting room has comfortable furniture, a fire and logs, and games and books aplenty; bedrooms are as neat as a pin. Borrow a boat to fish, roam the estate, play tennis. Pony trekking, white water rafting and golf are nearby. *More cottages available, one suitable for disabled guests with assistance.*

Price	£332-£616 per week. Please call for details.
Rooms	Cottage for 5 (1 double; 1 twin; 1 single).
Meals	Pub/restaurant 2 miles.
Closed	Never.
Directions	Directions given on booking.

Melanie MacIntyre
Kinloch Rannoch, Pitlochry PH16 5PD

Tel 0845 230 1491
Web www.dunalastair.com

Beinn Bhracaigh

Here is a solid Victorian villa, with later wings, built for an Edinburgh family in the 1880s, when Pitlochry was hailed as the Switzerland of the North. Ann and Alf, generous hosts, have swept through with the cream paint and all is spanking new. Expect soft lighting, gleaming wooden floors, silk flowers, bowls of pot pourri and scented candles. The lounge is comfy and has an honesty bar with over 50 malt whiskies, good-sized bedrooms have excellent mattresses, padded head boards and views to the Tummel Hills, bathrooms are all new with thick towels and lovely lotions. Breakfast is a huge, imaginative feast.

Price	£60-£90. Singles from £45.
Rooms	10: 4 doubles, 6 twins/doubles.
Meals	Dinner £22.50-£30 (for groups only, by arrangement). Pubs/restaurants 10-minute walk.
Closed	23-28 December.
Directions	From A9, turn for Pitlochry. Under railway bridge, then right at scout hut & up East Moulin Road. 2nd left into Higher Oakfield; house almost immediately on left.

Ann & Alf Berry
14 Higher Oakfield, Pitlochry, Perth PH16 5HT

Tel	01796 470355
Web	www.beinnbhracaigh.com

Killiecrankie House Hotel

Henrietta receives with great panache – no highland fling would be complete without a night or two at her extremely welcoming hotel. Outside are gardens galore; venture further afield and you come to Loch Tummel, Rannoch Moor and magnificent Glenshee. Return to a warm world of airy interiors: a little tartan in the dining room, 52 malts at the bar, views at breakfast of red squirrels. There's a snug sitting room where a fire burns, while doors open in summer for croquet on the lawn. Immensely comfortable bedrooms come in different shapes and sizes and have a smart country style. Spin down to the restaurant for delicious country fare. A super little place.

Price	Half-board £94-£114 p.p.
Rooms	10: 4 doubles, 4 twins/doubles, 2 singles.
Meals	Half-board only. Lunch from £3.50. Dinner for non-residents, £38.
Closed	January & February.
Directions	A9 north of Pitlochry, then B8079, signed Killiecrankie. Straight ahead for 2 miles. Hotel on right, signed.

Henrietta Fergusson
Killiecrankie, Pitlochry PH16 5LG

Tel 01796 473220
Web www.killiecrankiehotel.co.uk

Craigatin House & Courtyard

Pitlochry is a vibrant town with a theatre festival, castles, mountains, lochs and forests. This handsome house – now a chic B&B – is perfectly situated to explore it all. It stands peacefully in manicured gardens; good restaurants are a short stroll. Beautiful windows flood rooms with light, conservatory doors open to sun loungers on the terrace. Big uncluttered bedrooms – some in the main house, others in converted stables – are good value for money. Expect Farrow & Ball hues, comfy beds, crisp linen, padded bedheads and pretty shower rooms. Breakfast is the full cooked works with some tempting alternatives. It's on the Whisky Trail, too. *Minimum stay two nights at weekends.*

Price	£60-£90. Suite £100. Singles from £70.
Rooms	13: 10 doubles, 2 twins, 1 suite.
Meals	Restaurants in town.
Closed	Christmas.
Directions	A9 north to Pitlochry. Take 1st turn-off for town, up main street, past shops and signed on left.

Martin & Andrea Anderson
165 Atholl Road, Pitlochry PH16 5QL
Tel 01796 472478
Web www.craigatinhouse.co.uk

Craighall Castle

The view from the balcony that circles the drawing room is simply stunning, and the deep gorge provides the fabulous walks where you might glimpse deer, red squirrels and otters. Nicky and Lachie, ever welcoming, battle to keep up with the demands of the impressive home that has been in the family for 500 years. Any mustiness or dustiness can be forgiven, as staying here is a memorable experience. Nothing is contrived, sterile or luxurious, and there's so much drama and intrigue it could be the setting for a film. Breakfast is served in the 18th-century library, and there's a Regency drawing room, too.

Price	£80. Singles £45.
Rooms	2: 1 four-poster; 1 twin (extra single bed) with separate bath.
Meals	Restaurant 3 miles.
Closed	Christmas & New Year.
Directions	From Blairgowrie, A93 for Braemar for 2 miles. Just before end of 30mph limit, sharp right-hand bend, with drive on right. Follow drive for 1 mile.

Nicky & Lachie Rattray
Blairgowrie PH10 7JB

Tel 01250 874749
Email lrattray@craighall.co.uk

Forter Castle

Live out your highland fantasies in this 16th-century castle – a magnificent exclamation mark against Glenisla's wooded backdrop. Step into the Great Hall, its walls hung with portraits; the story of the family's renovation is almost as fascinating as the castle's history. From the grand Laird's Room to the (very cosy) bedrooms in the turrets, every detail is perfect. Cook in the small but beautifully equipped kitchen (the housekeeper provides a bespoke service, from fridge-stocking to personal chef); sink into exquisite beds at night. Walks and wildlife; a tiny chapel with a wedding licence; a castle fit for a royal party.

Price	£3,000-£4,200 per week.
Rooms	Castle for 12 (3 four-posters; 3 twins/doubles).
Meals	Chef available (£55 per person). Pub 6 miles.
Closed	Rarely.
Directions	Directions given on booking.

Sam Pooley
Glenisla, Blairgowrie PH11 8QW
Tel 07817 990784
Web www.fortercastle.com

Rock House

Prepare to fall hopelessly in love. Hard to know here, high above Loch Tay, whether the views are more beautiful outside or in. The cathedral ceiling in the sitting room allows light to soar upwards, there's a striking collection of modern art and an unfussy style: white sofas, painted furniture, and, here and there, a bit of quirky fun or a perfect antique. Sleep deeply in beds piled with linen cushions, soft woollen throws and cotton ticking, wake to grape and mint salad, Irish bread, kedgeree or anything else you want... Roland and Penny are passionate about their house, the land, and real food. *Self-catering cottages also available, call for details.*

Price	£100. Singles £80.
Rooms	2 doubles.
Meals	Dinner, 2-3 courses, £20-£30. Packed lunch £10. Pub/restaurant 2.2 miles.
Closed	Rarely.
Directions	From Aberfeldy, A827 dir. Kenmore. At Loch Tay where main road turns sharp right, cont. along narrow road signed Acharn. Follow loch side for 2.2 miles. At top of hill, house on right.

Roland & Penny Kennedy
Achianich, Kenmore, Aberfeldy PH15 2HU
Tel 01887 830336
Web www.lochtay.co.uk

The Ardeonaig Hotel & Restaurant

A bit of heaven on the quiet side of Loch Tay. This is a seriously spoiling hotel, the epitome of 21st-century country chic: whitewashed walls, hanging baskets, a courtyard where stone flower beds tumble with colour. Best of all: a library in varnished pine with a huge window framing views of field, loch and mountain. Expect plump sofas, leather armchairs, books, maps and binoculars; a snug bar in tartan, a peat fire, seriously good food. Stylish bedrooms are free of TVs and come with good art instead; those at the back have exquisite views. Stroll down to the water and find a flotilla of fishing boats – the hotel has rights, so bring a rod. *Minimum stay two nights at weekends.*

Price	£180-£300. Singles from £90. Lodges & suites from £350.
Rooms	27: 20 doubles, 5 lodges, 2 suites.
Meals	Bistro meals from £6.50. Dinner £26.50-£40. Tasting menu £49.50.
Closed	Never.
Directions	A9, then A827 to Kenmore via Aberfeldy. In Kenmore take south side road along Loch Tay for 10 miles. On right.

Pete Gottgens
Loch Tay, Killin FK21 8SU

Tel	01567 820400
Web	www.ardeonaighotel.co.uk

The Royal Hotel

The Royal is softly grand, intimate and welcoming, a country house in town. Queen Victoria once stayed, hence the name. Two fires burn side by side in a wonderful sitting room, newspapers hang on poles, logs tumble from baskets, sofas are impeccably upholstered. Eat at leather armchairs in the bar; on Lloyd Loom chairs in the conservatory/brasserie; and at smart tables in the dining room. Spotless rooms above have padded bedheads, crisp linen, mahogany dressers. Bathrooms come with fluffy robes, one four-poster has a log fire. Loch Tay, Pitlochry, The Trossachs and Perth are on your doorstep, even Edinburgh is easy to get to. Brilliant.

Price	£140. Four-posters £160. Singles from £85. Half-board £90-£110 p.p. Self-catering from £320 (2 nights).
Rooms	11 + 1: 5 doubles, 3 twins, 3 four-posters. 1 self-catering townhouse for 4.
Meals	Bar meals from £6.95. Dinner, 3 courses, £26.50.
Closed	Occasionally.
Directions	A9 N. of Dunblane; A822 thro' Braco & left onto B827. Left for town centre, over bridge; on square.

Teresa Milsom
Melville Square, Comrie PH6 2DN
Tel 01764 679200
Web www.royalhotel.co.uk

Monachyle Mhor

This 17th-century farmhouse is one of Scotland's coolest hotels. It's a family affair set in 2,000 acres of silence; the Trossachs circle around you, Loch Voil shimmers below. Step inside to find a slim restaurant behind a wall of glass, a candlelit bar, an open fire in the sitting room. Bedrooms – most in converted stone outbuildings – are dreamy: big beds, cool colours, hi-tech gadgets; bathrooms can be out of this world. Rooms in the main house are smaller, while suites in loft-house style are enormous. Dinner is five courses of unbridled heaven: beef, lamb, pork, venison, all off the farm. Walk, sail, fish, ride a bike through the forest. *Minimum stay two nights at weekends.*

Price	£105-£190. Singles from £95. Suites £180-£245. Half-board from £98.50 p.p.
Rooms	14: 3 doubles, 2 twins, 9 suites.
Meals	Sunday lunch £31. Dinner £46.
Closed	January.
Directions	M9 junc. 11, then B824 and A84 north. 6 miles north of Callander, turn right for Balquhidder. 5 miles west along road & Loch Voil. Hotel on right up drive, signed.

Tom Lewis
Balquhidder, Lochearnhead FK19 8PQ

Tel	01877 384622
Web	www.mhor.net

Creagan House

Where else can you sit in a baronial dining room and read up on the iconography of the toast rack while waiting for your bacon and eggs? Creagan is run with passion by Gordon and Cherry. Food is local – meat and game from Perthshire, seafood from west-coast boats – all served on Skye pottery. There's a snug sitting room which doubles as a bar with a good wine list and 50 malts. Bedrooms come with smart carpets, wood and florals, flat-screen TVs, a sofa if there's room. No airs and graces, just the attention you only get in small owner-run places. Bag a munro; let the sticks at the front door help you up Beinn An T-Sidhein. A perfect wee retreat.

Price	£120-£130. Singles £70-£85.
Rooms	5: 1 four-poster, 3 doubles, 1 twin.
Meals	Dinner, 3 courses, £29.50-£34.50.
Closed	Wednesdays, Thursdays & February.
Directions	From Stirling, A84 north through Callander to Strathyre. 0.25 miles north of village on right.

Gordon & Cherry Gunn
Strathyre, Callander FK18 8ND
Tel 01877 384638
Web www.creaganhouse.co.uk

Mackeanston House

They grow their own organic fruit, make their own preserves, bake their own bread. Likeable and energetic – Fiona a wine buff and talented cook, Colin a tri-lingual guide – your hosts are hospitable people whose 1690 farmhouse combines informality and luxury in peaceful, central Scotland. Light-filled bedrooms have soft carpets, pretty fabrics, fine antiques; one has a canopied bed, a double shower (with a seat if you wish it) and a bath that overlooks fields. In the conservatory with views to Stirling Castle you may dine on salmon from the Teith and game from close by. *Local & battlefield tours.*

Price	£92-£98. Singles £56-£59.
Rooms	2: 1 double, 1 twin/double.
Meals	Dinner £28. Pub 1 mile.
Closed	Christmas.
Directions	From M9, north, junc. 10 onto A84 for Doune. After 5 miles, left on B826 for Thornhill. Drive on left after 2.2 miles, right off farm drive.

Fiona & Colin Graham
Doune, Stirling FK16 6AX
Tel 01786 850213
Web www.mackeanstonhouse.co.uk

Old Kippenross

Pink since 1715 (a signal to Jacobites that the house was a safe haven), Old Kippenross rests in a wooden valley overlooking the river Allan – spot herons, dippers and otters. The Georgian part was built above the 500-year-old Tower House, and its rustic white-vaulted basement embraces dining room and sitting room, strewn with soft sofas and Persian rugs. Upstairs there are deeply comfortable sash-windowed bedrooms and warm, well-equipped bathrooms stuffed with towels. Sue and Patrick (who is an expert on birds of prey) are welcoming; breakfast and dinner are delicious. *Children over ten welcome. Dogs by arrangement.*

Price	£90. Singles from £60.
Rooms	2: 1 double, 1 twin.
Meals	Dinner £27. BYO. Pub 1.5 miles.
Closed	Rarely.
Directions	M9 exit 11, B8033 for Dunblane. 500 yds, right over dual c'way, thro' entrance by stone gatehouse. Down drive, 1st fork right after bridge. House along gravelled drive.

Sue & Patrick Stirling-Aird
Dunblane FK15 0LQ

Tel 01786 824048
Email kippenross@hotmail.com

An Lochan

This is one of Scotland's most famous inns. It was run for years by a Yorkshireman, these days it's safely back in Scottish hands – simplicity is the virtue. You get slate floors covered in hessian, logs piled in the fireplace, panelled walls, roaring fires, old beams running above. Weave into the restaurant to find whitewashed walls and wooden benches smartly upholstered in green tartan; double doors lead through to high ceilings and painted pine in the conservatory. Super food is served informally; expect to eat well. Homely bedrooms tend to be big. Gleneagles is ten miles north, tee times can be arranged.

Price	£100. Singles £85. Lodge £150.
Rooms	13: 12 twins/doubles, 1 lodge for 4.
Meals	Lunch from £7.95. Dinner, 3 courses, from £24.95.
Closed	Never.
Directions	A9 north from Dunblane, then A823 south at Gleneagles. On left in village.

Roger & Bea McKie
Glendevon FK14 7JY
Tel 0845 371 1414
Web www.anlochan.co.uk

Skirling House

An intriguing house with 1908 additions, impeccably maintained. The whole lovely place is imbued with the spirit of Scottish Arts & Crafts, augmented with Italianate flourishes. Colourful blankets embellish chairs; runners soften flagged floors; the carvings, wrought-ironwork and rare Florentine ceiling are sheer delight. Upstairs, a more English comfort holds sway: carpets and rugs, window seats and wicker, fruit and flowers. Bob cooks the finest local produce, Isobel shares a love of Scottish contemporary art and both look after you beautifully. Outside: 25,000 newly planted trees and grand walks from the door.

Price	£110-£120. Singles £60.
Rooms	5: 3 doubles, 1 twin, 1 twin/double.
Meals	Dinner £32. Pubs/restaurants 2 miles.
Closed	Christmas & January-February.
Directions	From Biggar, A702 for Edinburgh. Just outside Biggar, right on A72 for Skirling. Big wooden house on right opp. village green.

Bob & Isobel Hunter
Skirling, Biggar ML12 6HD
Tel 01899 860274
Web www.skirlinghouse.com

Windlestraw Lodge

There are few better distractions in Scotland than following the river Tweed; fishing lines glisten in the sun, lambs bleat high on the hill, ospreys glide through the sky. This supremely comfortable country house sits on the side of a hill with timeless views down the valley. A dazzling refurbishment has softened the grandness giving the feel of home: there are stripped floors, roaring fires, fat sofas, a panelled dining room, a terrace for afternoon tea, a sitting room for a snooze. Bedrooms are fine; two are sublime, all come with crisp linen, those at the front have the views. Don't miss Alan's fabulous food or golf at Peebles. Brilliant.

Price	£130-£180. Singles from £80. Half-board from £105 p.p.
Rooms	6: 5 doubles, 1 twin.
Meals	Lunch by arrangement. Dinner, 4 courses, £40.
Closed	Rarely.
Directions	East from Peebles on A72. Into Walkerburn; house signed left on western flank of town.

Julie & Alan Reid
Tweed Valley, Walkerburn EH43 6AA

Tel	01896 870 636
Web	www.windlestraw.co.uk

Over Langshaw Farm

A peaceful place in the rolling hills of the Scottish Borders, with an inspiring commitment to organic food and good husbandry. The energy here goes into Friesians and ewes, homemade farmhouse ice creams, bonny brown hens and guests. So, a cheery place for families and walkers, with unsophisticated bedrooms, old-fashioned bathrooms and a guest sitting room with a log fire and white shutters. Plus all the nooks and crannies you'd expect from a 1700s house, and a sweet smiling welcome from Sheila. She and Martyn have detailed walking maps and could not be more helpful. Authentic – and with views to die for. *Self-catering cottage available.*

Price	£65. Family room £75. Singles £35.
Rooms	2: 1 double; 1 family room with separate bath.
Meals	Dinner from £20. Packed lunch from £5. Pubs/restaurants 4-5 miles.
Closed	Never.
Directions	North from Galashiels, A7 past Torwoodlea golf course & right to Langshaw. After 2 miles, right at T-junc., then left at Earlston sign in Langshaw. White house, in trees, signed at farm road.

Sheila & Martyn Bergius
Galashiels TD1 2PE

Tel 01896 860244
Email overlangshaw@btconnect.com

Fauhope House

Near to Melrose Abbey and the glorious St Cuthberts' Walk, this solid 1890s house is immersed in bucolic bliss. Views soar to the Eildon Hills through wide windows with squashy seats; all is elegant, fire-lit, fresh and serene. Bedrooms are warm with deeply coloured walls, thick chintz, pale tartan blankets and soft carpet; bathrooms are modern and pristine. Breakfast is served with smiles at a flower-laden table and overlooking those purple hills. A short walk through the garden and over a footbridge takes you to the interesting town of Melrose, with shops, restaurants and its own theatre.

Price	From £80. Singles from £55.
Rooms	3 twins/doubles.
Meals	Pub/restaurant 0.5 miles.
Closed	Rarely.
Directions	From A7, through Gattonside; at end of village, at sign on left 'Monkswood', immed. left; right up drive.

Ian & Sheila Robson
Gattonside, Melrose TD6 9LY
Tel 01896 823184
Email fauhope@bordernet.co.uk

Oldhamstocks Cottage

In a tiny sleepy Scottish village, and opposite the owners' house, is this immaculately restored, one-storey cottage. You get a sunny sitting room, a well-equipped little kitchen, two comfy bedrooms with White Company linen, and a spotless bathroom. For winter there's a cosy coal fire with games and DVDs; for summer, a delightfully enclosed garden with table and chairs; its door leads to the village green and a small play park. Thanks to the unspoilt sandy beaches, the rolling Lammermuir Hills and the 19 fabulous golf courses, walkers and sporty types will love it here. Culture-seekers have Edinburgh, a 35-minute drive (or easy train ride).

Price	£290-£595 per week. Short breaks from £200.
Rooms	Cottage for 4 (1 double; 1 twin).
Meals	Pubs 7 miles.
Closed	Never.
Directions	Directions given on booking.

Olivia Reynolds
Oldhamstocks, Dunbar TD13 5XN
Tel 01368 830233
Web www.oldhamstockscottage.com

Lessudden

A treat to stay in a great and historic tower house in the heart of the Scottish Borders. Your generous hosts give you big cosy bedrooms with private bathrooms and a spacious sitting room with fine old rugs, heaps of books and a log fire. Memorable meals are served at a polished oak refectory table beneath the gaze of Sir Walter Scott's uncle and aunt; they lived here, he was a frequent visitor. The 1680s white-stone stairwell is unique, the décor is traditional and homely, the living is relaxed and Alasdair and Angela care for their guests as open-heartedly as they do their cats, dogs, horses and hens.

Price	From £70. Singles from £50.
Rooms	2: 1 double; 1 twin with separate bathroom.
Meals	Dinner, 3-4 courses, £25. Pub 0.5 miles.
Closed	Rarely.
Directions	North on A68 to St Boswells. Right opp. Buccleuch Arms Hotel, on through village; left up drive immed. beyond turning to golf course.

Alasdair & Angela Douglas-Hamilton
St Boswells TD6 0BH

Tel 01835 823244
Web www.lessudden.com

New Belses Farm

Once lost by Lord Lothian in a game of backgammon, this Georgian farmhouse is safe in current hands. Delightful Helen divides her time between helping on the farm, gardening and caring for sundry pets, fan-tail doves, hens (fox permitting), family and guests. Bedrooms glow in a harmony of old paintings, lush chintzes and beautiful antiques; beds are extra long, towels snowy white. It's like home, only better. Discover great Border towns, stunning abbeys, fishing on the Tweed. Enjoy an excellent dinner locally then back to plump sofas by the log fire. Heaven.

Price	From £80.
Rooms	2: 1 double, 1 twin.
Meals	Pubs/restaurants 3.5-5 miles.
Closed	Christmas.
Directions	From Jedburgh, A68 for Edinburgh. Left after 3.5 miles to Ancrum; B6400 Ancrum to Lilliesleaf road; right after 4 miles, down drive (signed).

Peter & Helen Wilson
Ancrum, Jedburgh TD8 6UR
Tel 01835 870472
Email wilson699@totalise.co.uk

Nether Swanshiel

In gorgeous, unspoilt border country, an easy drive from Edinburgh, a listed Georgian manse. Sylvia is an excellent hostess and cook: Aga-baked scones or gingerbread for tea, organic produce (when possible) for dinner, kippers, compotes and homemade bread for breakfast. You eat by the Victorian bay window in the guest sitting room and you sleep deeply in very private rooms, simply and softly furnished. Outside, the Aulds' organic methods are reaping rewards: the garden is alive with birds, bees and butterflies, yellow azaleas scent the spring, wild orchids flourish under the fruit trees, and martagon lilies pop up in unexpected places.

Price	£70. Single £35.
Rooms	3: 2 twins, each with separate bathroom; 1 single.
Meals	Dinner £20 (if staying min. 2 nights). Village pub 1 mile.
Closed	November–February.
Directions	B6357 or B6088 to Bonchester Bridge. Turn opp. pub (Horse & Hound). Beyond church 1st lane to right. Set back off road.

Dr Sylvia Auld
Hobkirk, Bonchester Bridge TD9 8JU
Tel 01450 860636
Web www.netherswanshiel.fsnet.co.uk

The Moss

Rozie loves fishing and Jamie keeps bees; they live in a charming listed house full of lovely things and are great hosts. Outside are 28 acres where deer prune the roses, pheasants roam and a garden seat sits with its toes in the water. Generous bedrooms are very private in their own wing and have big beds with feather pillows, books, flowers and long views to pastures and moorland. Expect walking sticks and the bell of HMS Tempest in the porch, rugs in the hall and smart sofas in the log-fired drawing room. Breakfast comes fresh from the Aga and is delivered to a big oak table, from which there are yet more views.

Price	£80. Singles £40.
Rooms	3: 1 twin; 2 doubles sharing bath (2nd room let to same party only).
Meals	Pubs/restaurants within 2 miles.
Closed	Rarely.
Directions	4 miles west of Blanefield. Half a mile after Beech Tree Inn turn left off A81. After 300 yds, over bridge, 1st entrance on left.

Jamie & Rozie Parker
Killearn G63 9LJ

Tel 01360 550053
Email themoss@freeuk.com

Duns Inane

The wild west wind has left its mark on this granite gem, giving it an undisputed authenticity, while the porch pulls you in from the windswept moor. Escape the pursuing boggarts and beasties in the once-cosy kitchen, now fashionably extended upwards to include the bedroom above, with views to the glowering sky. Owner Rusty McThatch once trod the boards of the Glasgow Empire, now he tends to fall through the ones here. It's comforting to hear him shout Macbeth's soliloquy in the dead of night from the cold cellar, while you snuggle safe under your horsehair blanket, by the light of a brief candle.

Price	Whatever the three sisters you meet at the crossroads ask.
Rooms	2 airy bedrooms.
Meals	Country pancakes a speciality.
Closed	Tomorrow and tomorrow and tomorrow.
Directions	Over the moor, then left at Birnam Wood.

Rusty McThatch
The Wild & Windy Moor, Glen Garyglenross
Tel 0666 666 666
Web www.whereonearth.ami

Ballat Smithy

A well cared for and well-equipped cottage – owned by Anne, so delighted to introduce you to this beautiful area. House, cottage, workshop and byre, at the side of the road, were built in 1830 as a smithy on the Buchanan estate; today the workshop is a delightfully solid, eco-friendly cottage. Views from the front are to the Campsie Fells. All is on one floor: walls are pastel, curtains terracotta, sofas are leather and sheets organic and Fair Trade – there's a patio with seating, too. Excellent shops and pubs are close, as are the 'bonnie banks' of Loch Lomond and the Trossachs National Park.

Price	£295-£450 per week.
Rooms	Cottage for 4 + cot (2 twins/doubles).
Meals	Pubs/restaurants 3 miles.
Closed	Never.
Directions	Directions given on booking.

Anne Currie
Balfron Station G63 0SE

Tel 01360 440269
Web www.ballatsmithycottage.com

Blairhullichan

So much to do here in the National Park: woodland walks, cycle tracks, your own fishing bay on the edge of Loch Ard, a private island to wade out to for picnics. The tranquil house sits high on a slope with fabulous loch views from the drawing room, comfortable with window bay, big fireplace and stacks of books. Reassuringly old-fashioned bedrooms have new mattresses and crisp linen; bathrooms have good towels and lotions. Be charmed by the 'Highlands in miniature' – plus resident labradors and welcoming Bridget, who gives you a grand breakfast and the best of her local knowledge. *Minimum stay two nights.*

Price	£75-£80. Singles £40.
Rooms	3: 1 double with sitting room, 1 twin; 1 double with separate bath/shower.
Meals	Dinner, with wine, £25-£35. Restaurant 10 miles.
Closed	Mid-December-mid-February.
Directions	A81 to Aberfoyle; at Bank of Scotland, onto B829 to Kinlochard; 4.5 miles, pass Macdonald Hotel into village. Left at shop onto unpaved road; pass new wooden house on right. On left, signed.

John & Bridget Lewis
Kinlochard, Aberfoyle FK8 3TN

Tel 01877 387341
Web www.blairhullichan.net

Blairhullichan, The Garden Wing

Blairhullichan has stood on the banks of Loch Ard for at least three centuries and you are in its oldest wing – the dining room dates from the 1600s and was once a game larder (note the hook in the ceiling). Awake to birdsong, soak in a roll top tub, breakfast in the sheltered courtyard – then plan your day. In the sitting room with wood-burning stove, games and books galore, is masses of information on where to go: Loch Lomond and Stirling Castle are close; Kinlochard's tea room and village store are a five-minute walk. Ramble in ancient oakwoods, cycle in the foothills of Ben Lomond, row – or wade – out to the Lewis's private loch island to picnic or fish. Lovely.

Price	£425-£750 per week.
Rooms	Wing of house for 7 (1 double; 1 twin; 1 triple).
Meals	Available on request.
Closed	Mid-January-mid-February.
Directions	A81 to Aberfoyle; at Bank of Scotland, onto B829 to Kinlochard; 4.5 miles, pass Macdonald Hotel into village. Left at shop onto unpaved road; pass new wooden house on right. On left, signed.

John & Bridget Lewis
Kinlochard, Aberfoyle FK8 3TN

Tel 01877 387341
Web www.blairhullichan.net

Cardross

Dodge the lazy sheep on the long drive to arrive (eventually!) at a sweep of gravel and lovely old Cardross, in a gorgeous setting with its 15th-century tower. Bang on the enormous old door and either Archie or Nicola (plus labradors and Jack Russells) will usher you in. And what a delight it is; light and space, long views, exquisite furniture, wooden shutters, towelling robes, fresh flowers, crisp linen, a cast-iron period bath – and that's just the bedrooms. It all feels warm, kind and generous, the drawing room is vast, the house is filled with character and the Orr Ewings can tell you all the history.

Price	£90-£100. Singles £50-£55.
Rooms	2: 1 twin; 1 twin with separate bath.
Meals	Occasional dinner. Pubs/restaurants 2.5-6 miles.
Closed	Christmas & New Year.
Directions	A811 Stirling-Dumbarton to Arnprior; B8034 towards Port of Menteith; 2 miles, then cross Forth over humpback bridge. Drive with yellow lodge 150 yds from bridge on right. 1st exit on right from drive.

Sir Archie & Lady Orr Ewing
Port of Menteith, Kippen FK8 3JY

Tel 01877 385223
Web www.cardrossholidayhomes.com

Ballochneck

This magical pile stands one mile up a rutted drive, soundproofed by 175 acres of lush Stirlingshire. Swans nest on the lake in spring, which doubles as a curling pond in winter, sheep graze and deer come to eat the rhododendrons. The house is still a home, albeit a grand one. Inside you get all the aristocratic works – roaring fires, painted panelling – but Donnie and Fiona are the real stars; expect a little banter, a few good stories. Vast bedrooms have huge views and beautiful beds. Breakfast is a feast, served in summer in a Victorian conservatory amid lavender and wandering clematis. *Children over 12 welcome. Minimum stay two nights at weekends.*

Price	£145-£160. With interconnecting twin £215.
Rooms	3: 1 double en suite; 1 double with private bathroom; 1 interconnecting twin (let to same party only).
Meals	Dinner, 4 courses, £35.
Closed	Christmas & New Year.
Directions	M9 junc. 10; A84 west, B8075 south, A811 to Buchlyvie. There, right for Aberfoyle. Over bridge, up to lodge house 200 yds on left. 1 mile up drive.

Donnie & Fiona Allan
Buchlyvie FK8 3PA

Tel 01360 850216
Web www.ballochneck.com

Kinloch

Meander across the flower-filled machair to the wide open spaces of South Uist – home to waders, hen harriers, corncrakes and talkative Wegg. The house, built 20 years ago, is comfy with books, photos, easy chairs, pictures and angling paraphernalia. Bedrooms – the upstairs double the best – have patchwork and pine and a general junk-shop chic; views across the loch are enormous, sunrises are spectacular. Wegg loves cooking, especially barbecued fish and game; his breakfasts and dinners are sociable occasions and you are surrounded by a clever acre of garden. Nature lovers will adore it. *Shoes off at the front door!*

Price	£66. Singles £33.
Rooms	3: 1 double/twin; 1 double/twin, 1 single sharing owner's bathroom.
Meals	Dinner £17. Packed lunch £6. Restaurant 5 miles.
Closed	Rarely.
Directions	30 mins from Benbecula airport; 30 mins from Lochboisdale ferry; 45 mins from Lochmaddy.

Wegg Kimbell
Grogarry, South Uist HS8 5RR
Tel 01870 620316
Web www.kinlochuist.com

Airdabhaigh

A rare 'undiscovered' corner of Britain… moody hills, lochs and acres of treeless blowy shores are wildly atmospheric. Miles of white sandy beaches too, and vast skies. Flora is inspirational; she's involved in Community Arts and runs dyeing and weaving workshops – a unique island experience. Wood panelling, thick walls, a peat fire, a warm kitchen, the wind whistling outside – and now, just below the house, a restored thatched shieling for writing, reading, painting. Sweet bedrooms are a haven of warmth and simplicity. It's utterly peaceful, 100% authentic, a step back in time. *Ask about creative workshops.*

Price	£40. Singles £22.
Rooms	2: 1 double, 1 twin sharing shower.
Meals	Pub/restaurant within walking distance.
Closed	Rarely.
Directions	From Lochmaddy ferry, left on A867 for 8.6 miles to T-junc. Left on A865 for 2.4 miles (ignore signs to Carinish), then right at church. Up track. House 1st on left.

Flora Macdonald
Uppertown, Carinish, North Uist HS6 5HL
Tel 01876 580611
Web www.calanas.co.uk

Tigh Dearg

This far-flung island chain is worth every second it takes to get here. Come for huge skies, sweeping beaches, carpets of wild flowers, stone circles, ancient burial chambers, white-tailed eagles. The house is a delight, immensely welcoming, full of colour, warmly contemporary, with windows that flood it with light. Swanky bedrooms, some under the eaves, come with suede headboards, power showers, bathrobes and beach towels, bowls of fruit and crisp linen. In the restaurant, lobster, crab, squid, sole all come straight from the water. Walk, ride, fish, canoe, then return and try the sauna. Come in November for the northern lights. Fabulous.

Price	£80-£145.
Rooms	8 twins/doubles.
Meals	Bar meals from £8.50. Dinner, 3 courses, £25-£30.
Closed	Never.
Directions	North into Lochmaddy. Left, signed Police Station. Hotel on left after 200 yds.

Iain MacLeod
Lochmaddy, North Uist HS6 5AE

Tel 01876 500700
Web www.tighdearghotel.co.uk

Scarista House

All you need to know is this: Harris is one of the most beautiful places in the world. Turquoise water and beaches of white sand that stretch for a mile are not uncommon. If you bump into another soul, it will be a delightful coincidence. The view from Scarista is simple and magnificent: field, ridge, beach, water, sky. Patricia and Tim's home is heaven: peat fires, rugs on painted wooden floors, books galore, old oak furniture. The golf club has left a set of clubs by the front door in case you wish to play; walking sticks and wellies too. The delightful staff may speak Gaelic, the food is exceptional. Peaceful and inspiring.

Price	£175-£199. Singles from £120.
Rooms	5: 3 doubles, 2 twins.
Meals	Dinner, 3 courses, £39.50. Packed lunch £5.50.
Closed	Christmas & February.
Directions	From Tarbert, A859, signed Rodel. Scarista 15 miles on left, after golf course.

Patricia & Tim Martin
Isle of Harris HS3 3HX
Tel 01859 550238
Web www.scaristahouse.com

Broad Bay House

In a wild landscape, 21st-century sophistication and style. Built in 2007, the house rises on graceful flights of decking above the beach. On an otherwise deserted shore, there is a villa right next door – but it disappears the moment you're inside. A stunning hall leads to a vaulted living room, whose windows face the waves on three sides... wow! More intimate boutique hotel than B&B – subtle lighting, oak doors, original art – Broad Bay has been designed with sheer, unadulterated comfort in mind. Ian and Marion are considerate, generous, flexible hosts and the food, served at candlelit tables, is heavenly.

Price	£129-£170.
Rooms	4: 2 doubles, 2 twins/doubles.
Meals	Dinner, 3 courses, £30. Packed lunch £7-£10. Pub/restaurant 7 miles.
Closed	Rarely.
Directions	A867 from Stornoway towards Barvas & Ness. On edge of Stornoway, right onto B895. After 6 miles, house on right, between Back & Gress.

Ian Fordham
Back, Stornoway HS2 0LQ
Tel 01851 820990
Web www.broadbayhouse.co.uk

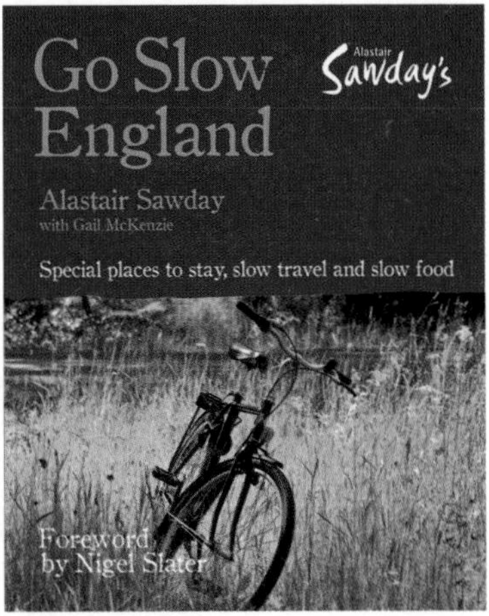

Special places to stay, slow travel and slow food

The Slow Food revolution is upon us and this guide celebrates the Slow philosophy of life with a terrific selection of the places, recipes and people who take their time to enjoy life at its most enriching. In this beautiful book that goes beyond the mere 'glossy', you will discover an unusual emphasis on the people who live in Special Slow Places and what they do. You will meet farmers, literary people, wine-makers and craftsmen – all with rich stories to tell. Go Slow England celebrates fascinating people, fine architecture, history, landscape and real food. A counter-balance to our culture of haste.

Written by Alastair Sawday, with a foreword by Nigel Slater.

RRP £19.99 To order at the Readers Discount price of £13.00 (plus p&p) call 01275 395431 and quote 'Reader Discount SCO'.

Special Places to Stay series

Have you enjoyed this book? Why not try one of the others in the Special Places to Stay series and get 35% discount on the RRP *

British Bed & Breakfast (Ed 13)	RRP £14.99	Offer price £9.75
British Bed & Breakfast for Garden Lovers (Ed 4)	RRP £14.99	Offer price £9.75
British Hotels & Inns (Ed 10)	RRP £14.99	Offer price £9.75
Devon & Cornwall (Ed 1)	RRP £ 9.99	Offer price £6.50
Scotland (Ed 1)	RRP £ 9.99	Offer price £6.50
Pubs & Inns of England & Wales (Ed 5)	RRP £14.99	Offer price £9.75
Ireland (Ed 6)	RRP £12.99	Offer price £8.45
French Bed & Breakfast (Ed 10)	RRP £15.99	Offer price £10.40
French Holiday Homes (Ed 4)	RRP £14.99	Offer price £9.75
French Hotels & Châteaux (Ed 5)	RRP £14.99	Offer price £9.75
Paris Hotels (Ed 6)	RRP £10.99	Offer price £7.15
Italy (Ed 5)	RRP £14.99	Offer price £9.75
Spain (Ed 7)	RRP £14.99	Offer price £9.75
Portugal (Ed 4)	RRP £11.99	Offer price £7.80
Croatia (Ed 1)	RRP £11.99	Offer price £7.80
Greece (Ed 1)	RRP £11.99	Offer price £7.80
Turkey (Ed 1)	RRP £11.99	Offer price £7.80
Morocco (Ed 2)	RRP £11.99	Offer price £7.80
India (Ed 2)	RRP £11.99	Offer price £7.80
Green Places to Stay (Ed 1)	RRP £13.99	Offer price £9.10
Go Slow England	RRP £19.99	Offer price £13.00

*postage and packing is added to each order

To order at the Reader's Discount price simply phone 01275 395431 and quote 'Reader Discount SCO'

If you have any comments on entries in this guide, please tell us. If you have a favourite place or a new discovery, please let us know about it. You can return this form to SCO, Sawday's, The Old Farmyard, Yanley Lane, Long Ashton, Bristol BS41 9LR, UK or visit www.sawdays.co.uk.

Existing entry

Property name: ______________________________

Entry number: ______________ Date of visit: ______________

New recommendation

Property name: ______________________________

Address: ______________________________

Tel/Email/Website: ______________________________

Your comments

What did you like (or dislike) about this place? Were the people friendly? What was the location like? What sort of food did they serve?

____

____

____

Your details

Name: ______________________________

Address: ______________________________

______________ Postcode: ______________

Tel: ______________ Email: ______________

Wheelchair-accessible

At least one bedroom and bathroom accessible for wheelchair users. Phone for details.

Argyll & Bute
12 • 21
Dumfries & Galloway
41
Dunbartonshire
46
Edinburgh & the Lothians
51
Fife
71 • 73
Highland
80 • 85 • 93 • 98
Perth & Kinross
119 • 125 • 126 • 129
Scottish Borders
130
Western Isles
147 • 149

National Cycle Network

These Special Places are within 2 miles of the NCN. (See www.sustrans.org.uk for details of routes.)

Angus
9
Argyll & Bute
18 • 22 • 23 • 24
Ayrshire
28 • 29 • 30
Dumfries & Galloway
40 • 43 • 44
Dunbartonshire
46
Edinburgh & the Lothians
47 • 48 • 49 • 50 • 51 • 52 • 53 • 54 • 56 • 57 • 58 • 59 • 60 • 61 • 62 • 63 • 64 • 68
Fife
69 • 70 • 75
Highland
77 • 78 • 81 • 82 • 83 • 84 • 85 • 86 • 107
Moray
111 • 112
Orkney
114
Perth & Kinross
117 • 118 • 119 • 122 • 123 • 126
Scottish Borders
130 • 131 • 133 • 135 • 136

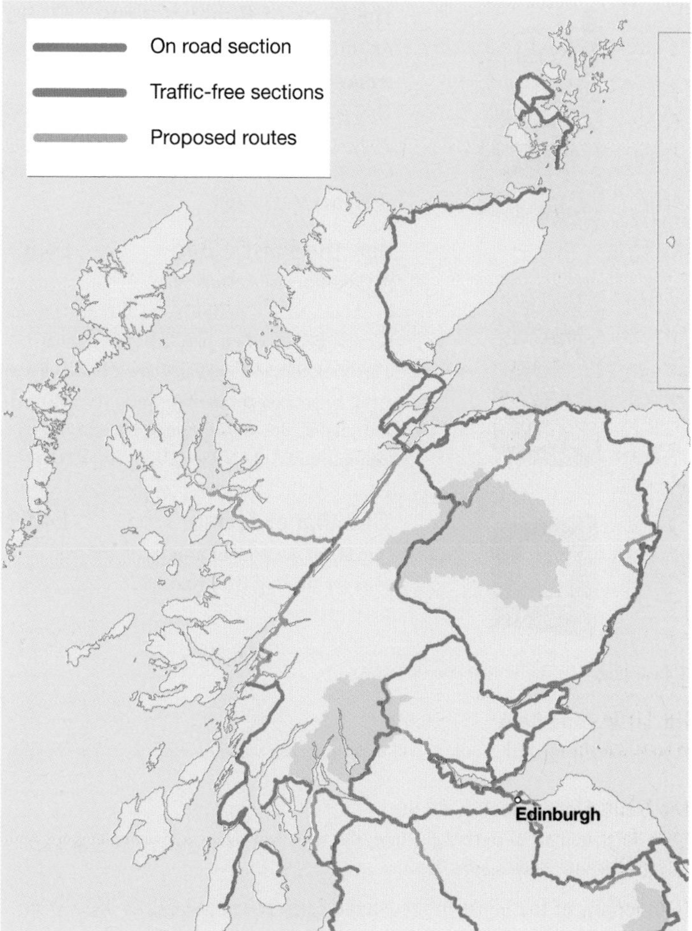
On road section
Traffic-free sections
Proposed routes
Edinburgh

The Big Earth Book

Updated paperback edition
£12.99

We all know the Earth is in crisis. We should know that it is big enough to sustain us if we can only mobilise politicians and economists to change course now. Expanding on the ideas developed in *The Little Earth Book*, this book explores environmental, economic and social ideas to save our planet. It helps us understand what is happening to the planet today, exposes the actions of corporations and the lack of action of governments, weighs up new technologies, and champions innovative and viable solutions. Tackling a huge range of subjects – it has the potential to become the seminal reference book on the state of the planet – it's the one and only environmental book you really need.

What About China? £6.99

Answers to this and other awkward questions about climate change

"What is the point of doing anything when China opens a new power station every week?"

All of us are guilty of making excuses not to change our lifestyles especially when it comes to global warming and climate change. *What About China?* explains that all the excuses we give to avoid making changes that will reduce our carbon footprint and our personal impact on the environment, are exactly that, excuses! Through clear answers, examples, facts and figures the book illustrates how any changes we make now will have an effect, both directly and indirectly, on climate change.

1 Dumfries & Galloway

2 Self-catering

3 West Holmhead Cottage, Craig Farm

4 This forgotten corner of Scotland is blissfully empty – red squirrels, kites and otters are its reclusive residents. Among hills and forests is a bio-dynamic farm run by Richard and Mas; 450 acres flourish naturally, orchids, mushrooms, ancient woodland are pasture for cattle and sheep. Your spotless white-painted stone cottage (one of two on a quiet lane) has a down-to-earth feel that echoes the owners' values – furniture is simple but not cheap, beds are pine, walls creamy white. Books and fresh flowers welcome, local walks are described in detail on handwritten cards. To be surrounded by such raw beauty is a balm to every soul.

5	Price	£300-£500 per week.
6	Rooms	Cottage for 5 (1 double; 1 twin; 1 single).
7	Meals	Pub 4 miles.
8	Closed	Rarely.
9	Directions	Directions given on booking.

10

Mas Smyth & Richard Cunningham
Balmaclellan, Castle Douglas DG7 3QR

Tel 01644 420636
Web www.craigfarm.co.uk

11 Entry 39 Map 2